A Best Book of 2015 Pick according to:

Elizabeth Gilbert

Michelle Obama

The Wall Street Journal, as selected by Dominique Crenn

BrainPickings

PBS Newshour

The Millions

Publisher's Marketplace

The New Yorker

Library Journal

People.com

Shelf Awareness

The Root

Newsday

NPR.org

Boston Globe

St. Louis Dispatch

Publishers Weekly

The Guardian

The Huffington Post

Praise for Elizabeth Alexander's
THE LIGHT OF THE WORLD

"A brave and beautiful book about love and loss—the deep pain that comes with such a loss, and the redemptive realization that such pain is a small price to pay for such a love."
—Jeannette Walls, *New York Times* bestselling author of *The Glass Castle*

"This is a gorgeous love story, written by one of America's greatest contemporary poets. Graceful in its simplicity, sweeping in scope, this book is proof that behind the boarded-up windows of America's roiled marriages and ruined affairs, true love still exists, and where it does exist, it graces the world— and us—with light and hope. Elizabeth Alexander is a prose writer of deep talent and affecting skill. With ease, she peels back layer after layer to show the soft secrets of affection, the kindness, and the wide open generosity of a full-hearted man and talented artist, who had more love to give in his relatively short lifetime than most of us will ever know."
—James McBride, National Book Award–winning author of *The Good Lord Bird* and #1 *New York Times* bestseller *The Color of Water*

"This is a beautifully written, heartrendingly candid account of the abrupt loss of her husband by the distinguished poet Elizabeth Alexander. It is a vivid, intensely rendered elegy of a remarkable man—husband, father, artist, chef. Both a memoir and a portrait of a marriage, THE LIGHT OF THE WORLD is, as its title suggests, a bittersweet testament to love and the memory of love, one of the most compelling memoirs of loss that I have ever read."

—Joyce Carol Oates, author of
A Garden of Earthly Delights and
National Book Award-winner *Them*

"Elizabeth Alexander paints such a vivid and beautiful portrait of her husband that the reader can't help but fall in love with him, and when he dies we are there to mourn him as well. In this way Elizabeth Alexander lets us see the world through her eyes. This book, her vision, his life—they are all extraordinary gifts."

—Ann Patchett

"In this powerful, beautifully written memoir, she shares the tragic story of her husband's sudden death, the challenges of raising her boys in the midst of gripping sorrow and the solace she gained along the road to healing."

—Michelle Obama,
More Magazine

"It is a sign of love."

—*New York Times Book Review*

"A tale of beautiful people who made a beautiful life together."
—*Los Angeles Review of Books*

"THE LIGHT OF THE WORLD is as beautiful and moving as a gorgeous piece of music. The minute I finished it, I longed to read it again."
—Anna Deavere Smith, award-winning playwright and actor

"Love—for a marvelous man, for her sons, for the textures and pleasures of the world—shines on every page of Elizabeth Alexander's THE LIGHT OF THE WORLD. This acutely observed study of what it means to lose one's beloved is a profound and beautiful contradiction: a joyous book that faces head-on the deepest grief, written with art and courage, and with limitless heart."
—Mark Doty, National Book Award-winner of *Fire to Fire*

"A radiant book of love's everlastingness and art's infinite sustenance."   —*Booklist* (starred review)

"THE LIGHT OF THE WORLD is an absolutely luminous read, the kind full of incompressible dimension best experienced in its totality."
—*Brain Pickings*

"A celebration of love, life, books, family, food and friends."
—*Tallahassee Democrat*

"In art, in poetry and in her community of friends and family, Alexander finds divinity. The memoir itself is, of course, art. Its eloquent, grief-struck gratitude draws the reader in, and we celebrate and mourn alongside Alexander."

—*Miami Herald*

"[Elizabeth Alexander] is gifted with an incredible ability to put words to meter and create profound meaning."

—*The Root*

"[In THE LIGHT OF THE WORLD, Elizabeth Alexander] tells a love story that is, itself, a story of loss."

—*WAMC Northeast Radio*

"The book is a testament to ardor, and also to profound loss."

—*Valley News*

"Beautiful, warm, lyrical, honest and reverent, THE LIGHT OF THE WORLD is a loving tribute to a much-loved husband, and to the strength, tenacity and determination of the wife left behind."

—*Winnipeg Free Press*

"Alexander relays the story of her husband's sudden death and how her grief affected her. Using her gift for words, however, she was able to find meaning in her loss"

—*BookReporter*

The Light of the World

A MEMOIR

Elizabeth Alexander

GRAND CENTRAL
PUBLISHING

NEW YORK   BOSTON

Grand Central Publishing
Hachette Book Group
1290 Avenue of the Americas
New York, NY 10104
grandcentralpublishing.com
twitter.com/grandcentralpub

Originally published in hardcover and ebook by Grand Central Publishing in April 2015
First Trade Paperback Edition: September 2016

Grand Central Publishing is a division of Hachette Book Group, Inc.
The Grand Central Publishing name and logo is a trademark of Hachette Book Group, Inc.

The publisher is not responsible for websites (or their content) that are not owned by the publisher.

The Hachette Speakers Bureau provides a wide range of authors for speaking events. To find out more, go to www.hachettespeakersbureau.com or call (866) 376-6591. [delete if author doesn't participate]

Library of Congress Cataloging-in-Publication Data has been applied for.

ISBN: 978-1-4555-9986-8 (trade paperback)

Printed in the United States of America

LSC-C

10 9 8 7 6 5 4 3

For Solomon and Simon,
who walk their father's walk

*"There is light within a person of light,
and it lights up the whole universe. If it does
not shine, there is darkness."*
—The Gospel According to Thomas

"O beauty, you are the light of the world!"
—Derek Walcott, "The Light of the World"

". . . the light insists on itself in the world"
—Lucille Clifton
"the light that came to lucille clifton"

Contents

I

"LAST NIGHT ON EARTH"

One

The story seems to begin with catastrophe but in fact began earlier and is not a tragedy but rather a love story. Perhaps tragedies are only tragedies in the presence of love, which confers meaning to loss. Loss is not felt in the absence of love. "The queen died and then the king died" is a plot, wrote E. M. Forster in *The Art of the Novel*, but "The queen died and then the king died of grief" is a story.

It begins on a beautiful April morning when a man wakes exhausted and returns to sleep in his beloved thirteen-year-old son's trundle bed, declaring, "This is the most comfortable bed I have ever slept in!" Or it begins when the wife says goodbye to the man a few hours later, walking in front of his car switching her hips a bit, a blown kiss as she heads to her office and he continues on to his painting studio.

Or the story begins as he packs a tote bag with the usual slim thermos of strong coffee made in an Italian stovetop moka pot, a larger thermos of cold water, two tangerines, a package of Nat Sherman MCD cigarettes, and a plastic sack of raw almonds. The tote is astral blue and printed with Giotto angels. Off to his studio for a day of painting, then home—as if nothing extraordinary has happened, when in fact he has been envisioning worlds—hanging the Giotto bag on a hook in the mudroom and changing out of his paint-splattered jeans into gym shorts and a T-shirt for yoga in the family room or a run on the treadmill in the basement.

Soon the two children will walk down Edgehill Road from the bus stop like burros under their knapsacks, and his wife will prepare dinner while listening to Thelonious Monk's evocative open intervals and sipping from a glass of white wine that he's opened and poured for her. "My frosty white?" she'd ask a few times a week, and he'd chuckle and say, "Right away, my love. Chop chop." They enjoyed playing, and acting out boy-girl courtliness. The thirteen-year-old does his homework and the twelve-year-old practices his drumming. The man's home life is the unchanging beautiful same, so anything could occur in the painting studio each day.

I am the wife. I am the wife of fifteen years. I am the plumpish wife, the pretty wife, the loving wife, the smart wife, the American wife. I am eternally his wife.

Perhaps the story begins with the three dozen lottery tickets he bought two days before he died, which I discovered weeks later, when they fluttered out of the pages of one of the many books he was reading.

Or it begins with his surprise fiftieth birthday party, four days before he died, and the spoken tributes from his loved ones, and strawberries and pancakes and music the next morning.

Or it began when I met him, sixteen years before. That was always a good story: an actual *coup de foudre*, a bolt of lightning, love at first sight. I felt a visceral torque, I would tell people, a literal churn of my organs: not butterflies, not arousal; rather, a not-unpleasant rotation of my innards, as never before. Lightning struck and did not curdle the cream but instead turned it to sweet, silken butter. Lightning turned sand into glass.

The story began in the winter of 1961, when two quietly mighty women were each pregnant, one in Asmara, Eritrea, and the other in Harlem, USA; one with her sixth child, one with her first.

The East African son would arrive on March 21, 1962, the most hallowed day of the zodiac. It is the beginning and the end of the astrological calendar, and so it is said that children born on March 21 are ancient souls who possess the wonder and innocence of newborns.

The American child, a girl, would come on May 30, into the chatter and buzz of Gemini, in Gotham.

Two

When Ficre Ghebreyesus and I met in New Haven in the late spring of 1996, the first thing he wanted to do was show me his art. He was living at the time at 218 State Street, the New Haven Cash Register Company building, in an unfinished loft where he slept and painted when he was not cooking his Eritrean fantasia food in the kitchen of Caffé Adulis, the restaurant he owned and ran with his brothers Gideon and Sahle. The restaurant was named in homage to Adulis, an ancient port city on the Red Sea that is now an archaeological excavation site, one of Africa's great "lost cities." Pliny the Elder was the first writer to mention Adulis, which he called "city of free men."

In those days Ficre used to chef through the evening, close down the restaurant, then paint until dawn in that loft, with its salvaged Steinway piano, a clothing rack he'd rolled down the street from Macy's when it went out of business and used as a closet for his few hanging garments, and graffiti scrawled by a previous occupant on the heavy metal door that read, "Foster Kindness."

There were paintings everywhere, mostly large dark canvases lit with brilliant corners of insistent life. The paintings gave a sense of his beloved homeland in wartime—the Eritrean War of Independence began shortly before he was born—infused with the light of determined humanity that would not be deferred or extinguished. He showed me pastel drawings with the driving color concerns that echoed Eritrean textile work and basketry as well as Matisse's sky-lit hues. There were linocuts and mono-prints he'd made at the Printmaking Workshop with master teacher Bob Blackburn, and paintings he'd made while studying at the Art Students League with Joseph Stapleton, one of the last of the Abstract Expressionists then teaching. Ficre made that art during New York years in which he was mostly working as a young people's leader and activist on behalf of Eritrean issues. And then there were portfolios of photographs—some of which would be exhibited at an office building of the U.S. Congress that summer—which told stories of Eritrea and its uncannily resilient people in saturated, painterly colors.

As Ficre showed me work he talked about his family: his late father, Gebreysus Tessema, a judge so ethical he was exiled hundreds of miles away from home when he refused to tamper with his judicial decisions to suit the wishes of the dictator and his minions. He adhered to many formalities and customs, Ficre said, but also loved his children—seven in total, one, Kebede, lost to war, Ficre at the number-six position—to climb on him and laugh when all would come home from work and school for the midday meal.

His mother, Zememesh Berhe, also navigated the family ship through the vagaries of war. She came from a clan of many sisters and two brothers, respected and tough Coptic Christian highlanders, who all raised their children near each other until war scattered them and took some of their lives. Mama Zememesh had Parkinson's disease, he told me that first day, and all of his siblings—Tadu, Mehret, Sara, Gideon, and Sahle, then in Addis Ababa, Nairobi, and New Haven—doted on her as she moved from one family constellation to the next. Their language was Tigrinya, an Afro-Asiatic tongue derived from the ancient South Semitic Ge'ez and spoken in Eritrea and its diaspora. His full name, Ficremariam Ghebreyesus, means "lover of Mary" and "servant of Jesus." The abbreviated "Ficre," as he was called, means "love."

Our love began in an instant and progressed inevitably. When Solomon Kebede Ghebreyesus, our first son, was born in April of 1998, we moved to 45 Livingston Street in New Haven. Ficre continued to invent and cook at Adulis. The great food writer and old-school newspaperman R. W. Apple visited the restaurant and after tasting Ficre's creations asked, in his article in the *New York*

Times, "A Culinary Journey Out of Africa and into New Haven":

"Is all this authentic?" ...

"Tricky word, authentic," [Ficre] replied. "Tricky idea. Food ideas move around the world very quickly today, and if you went to Eritrea, you'd find American touches here and there. There are thousands of Eritreans living in the United States, and when they go home, they take new food ideas with them. For us, that's no more foreign than pasta once was."

Adulis was a gathering place where people ate food they'd never imagined and learned about the culture and history of a country that most of them had never heard of. Ficre created legendary dishes such as shrimp barka that existed nowhere in Eritrea but rather in his own inventive imagination. Women called for it from St. Raphael's and Yale-New Haven Hospitals after they'd delivered their babies; people said they literally dreamed of it, a fairy food that tasted like nothing else. Here is how you make it:

SHRIMP BARKA

Time: 30 minutes

SERVES: 4

INGREDIENTS

4 tablespoons olive oil
3 medium red onions, thinly sliced

4 to 6 cloves garlic, minced

5 very ripe and juicy tomatoes, chopped coarsely

Salt and freshly ground black pepper, to taste

½ cup finely chopped fresh basil (1 bunch)

15 pitted dates (½ cup), cut crosswise in thirds

3 tablespoons unsweetened shredded coconut

½ cup half-and-half

1 pound medium shrimp (16 to 20), shelled and deveined

⅔ cup grated Parmesan cheese

2½ cups cooked basmati rice

INSTRUCTIONS

1. In a large, heavy pot, heat olive oil over medium heat. Add onions, and sauté until wilted, about 10 minutes. Add garlic, and continue sautéing, stirring frequently to prevent sticking, for 2 minutes longer. Stir in the tomatoes, salt, and pepper. Cover, and cook for about 5 minutes.

2. Add basil, dates, and coconut, and reduce heat to medium-low. Cook, uncovered, stirring occasionally, for 5 more minutes. Add the half-and-half, cover, and cook for 3 minutes.

3. Add shrimp to sauce. Cook, covered, until shrimp turns pink, about 5 minutes. Stir in the cheese, and then the rice, and serve immediately.

In the mornings before Ficre went to the restaurant, he painted in a garage studio behind our house. There his practice and colors changed. He moved more fully into his brilliantly abstracted space; figures, landscapes, and icons were discernible but not strictly representational. With this work, he applied and was admitted to the Yale School of Art.

Ficre's time in art school was a mixed bag. He was a "grown-up," extremely open to learning, as ever, but also not a malleable kid. He was a respected town professional and, by that time, a father of two after the arrival of Simon Alexander Ghebreyesus in 1999. His particular African diaspora aesthetics were sometimes mis-read by teachers—"Where are your African colors?" one asked (to our quiet amusement), perhaps noting the absent combination of red, black, and green. But he had a good experience as a teaching assistant for Richard Lytle—who had taught the class "Color" for decades in the manner of his friend and mentor, the painter and color theorist Josef Albers—and strong, honest encouragement from Sam Messer, a Brooklyn artist known for his collaborations with writers.

Ficre loved outdoor painting excursions in New Haven's mixed-metaphor landscape of New England trees and industrial detritus. He made some fascinating text-based pieces in class with conceptualist Mel Bochner. Most important, however, were some artist's visits to the school. He had an expansive studio visit from the painter Amy Sillman, whose use of color and commitment to abstraction spoke powerfully to Ficre. Having Adrian Piper and Martin Puryear in his studio was a highlight of his time in graduate school. He revered each artist as a true master and had worked with his classmates to arrange the visits. Though his work looked nothing like either one's, Piper and Puryear asked him the deep questions that took his practice to the next level. It especially pleased him that Piper practiced yogic headstands during her visit in his studio, for he was beginning his own devoted yoga practice around that time. He cared deeply that people come in peace, for he himself was a profoundly peaceful and peace-loving person, forged in the crucible of war.

Ficre was shy about his artwork. He wasn't a schmoozer. He loved to have certain visitors in his studio, but the marketplace was not for him. Dozens and dozens of friends in and out of the art world urged him to show and sell and literally begged to buy paintings and photographs. He was never quite ready, he mostly said, still finishing, still perfecting. It made me crazy, for I believed fervently in the beauty and power of what he made and wanted him to have an art career commensurate with his talent and output. "People will know this work after I'm gone, sweetie," he would say. He said it with a laugh, but he meant it. I don't suggest he thought he would leave this earth prematurely, but I do think he had faith in the long-run, and the lasting power of art, and that he also clearly knew what was his and his alone to accomplish. He understood that *ars longa, vita brevis*, no matter when you die.

Three

The story begins on a Thursday night. I bring an unexpected guest home to stay with us, an artist friend who'd spoken on campus that afternoon. When I take her to her hotel after dinner we find that it is in a deserted corner of town far off the beaten track, so I offer to bring her to sleep in our guest room. She accepts with relief, and I call Ficre to let him know company is coming.

When Lorna and I arrive home ten minutes later the house is lit and glowing. The kettle is hot and tea is brewing in the black Japanese cast-iron pot. Ficre has put raw almonds in a small, celadon bowl. It is late; the boys are sleeping.

We are so pleased to live like this, organized and open and welcome when friends pass through and we can bring them to Hamden, the hamlet adjacent to New Haven where we recently moved to live in a tan stucco Arts and Crafts–style house surrounded by a magic garden. Hamden, my first suburb, albeit a very urban one. Hamden, where Ficre fell in love with property that reminded him of the African "compound" where he grew up amidst flowers, inside walls his mother painted apricot, spring sky blue, rose violet, and butter yellow.

The next morning, I organize the children for school and send them off and Ficre makes coffee when our friend rises shortly after. We three drink our cappuccinos under the gazebo, which he'd painted in the delicate colors of the remembered borders of his mother's gauzy dresses and shawls. Some might take the colors for straightforward pastels, or Monet water lilies, but they came from Africa, and from his mother. Hanging inside the gazebo is a mobile he fashioned from some slender, twisty branches that blew down in the yard after a storm. The mobile turns gently in the breeze. The morning is gray, and the yard smells of the fresh, damp earth of early spring.

As we walk toward the house, something makes us look back into the yard over our shoulders. There is a giant hawk sitting on the branch of our hundred-year-old oak tree, eviscerating and devouring a squirrel.

We freeze to watch. The raptor is utterly focused on its task. I watch Ficre and Lorna scrutinizing, their artist's eyes recording what they see. The hawk attends to its business undisturbed. It is rapacious; it takes what it wants. The bloody ribbons of the squirrel's entrails hang off the branch as the hawk eats the entire remains of the hapless rodent in about five minutes.

Ficre tells us he has seen the bird the day before, with the children, and shows us a short video he took on his phone of the creature on the same branch, eating another squirrel. I have seen a hawk a few times but never one so intent on its survival, never seen predation itself up close and in action. It is pure and elemental, necessarily violent, riveting, nature itself. We watch for as long as we can before we have to go off to the duties of our days.

Some weeks later, on his bureau, I find an acrostic Ficre made, which exhausted variations on the word *hawk*. He'd assigned numbers to the letters and then assigned those numbers to lottery tickets, which I later discover he bought by the dozens and secreted in the pages of the books he was reading.

Four

Ficre was born in East Africa in Asmara, Eritrea's capital, in the midst of a three-decade-long war with Ethiopia for independence. There the story begins. Almost every family lost a child during those long war years. Ficre's eldest brother, Kebede, was always described as "a freedom fighter who fell in battle." The dictator Mengistu Haile Mariam's "Red Terror" claimed legions of young people in Eritrea and Ethiopia—500,000, by Amnesty International's final count—and years later he was convicted of genocide in absentia while in protected exile provided by Robert Mugabe in Zimbabwe.

Ficre's parents' bravery was in constant evidence in those years. They faced down soldiers who broke into their home while the children hid in the bedroom, and when Ficre was a teenager his mother retrieved him from the front lines where he'd gone to enlist and promptly arranged for him to leave the country. So at sixteen, Ficre was a refugee, first in Sudan, then Italy, then Germany, and finally in the United

States at the age of nineteen, in San Jose, New York City, and then, for almost thirty years, in the perhaps unlikely place of New Haven, Connecticut.

Before he came to this country, Ficre was exposed to U.S. black power rhetorics—an early visual icon for him was Angela Davis's luminous Afro—and thinkers such as Martinican Frantz Fanon. Black soul music from Sam Cooke to James Brown rocked in his head along with Fela Kuti's Afro-beat and Bob Marley's reggae. Thus culturally he was a global diasporist, a "conscious synchretist," in his own words. He was proudly and resolutely Eritrean, East African, and African. At the same time, he was unambiguous about being a black Eritrean American.

In a 2000 artist's statement, Ficre told his story and described himself and his creative influences:

"I started painting ten years ago, but I suspect I have been metaphorically doing so all my life. When I started painting, I just did it. I had never felt a stronger urge. The pieces that flowed out of me were very painful and direct. They had to do with the suffering, persecution, and subsequent psychological dilemmas I endured before and after becoming a young refugee from the Independence War.... Painting was the miracle, the final act of defiance through which I exorcised the pain and reclaimed my sense of place, my moral compass, and my love for life."

His statement continued:

"Asmara is a beautiful city at eight thousand feet above

sea-level, planned and designed by Italian colonialists at the turn of the century. In addition to the collision of architectures, iconographies, and propaganda art there was the unique, and palpable visual aesthetic of death: Soviet tanks rumbled through the streets, fighter planes strafed the skies, and deadly uniformed soldiers rummaged through the streets. It was a medieval vision of hell incarnate. Government-sponsored death squads had 'powers of emergency' over any Eritrean citizen. I suspect I have carried this angst and fear of imminent explosion within me to this day, for when I paint I am accompanied by dissonances, syncopations, and the ultimate will for life and moral order of goodness."

New York was a huge influence on him, as with so many artists before and after. Joseph Stapleton at the Art Students League was a connection to both Abstract Expressionism and the social realist history so prevalent at the League. He also worked for a time at the Cinque Gallery, where, if he were not before, he would have become familiar with Hale Woodruff's work and the great tradition of Woodruff's peers such as Charles Alston and Romare Bearden.

Beginning in 1996, Ficre's work underwent a profound transition of palette and aim, into a period of brilliant abstraction that is concomitant with his work developing and inventing recipes and ambiance at Caffé Adulis. He described the cultural influence of Eritrea on his aesthetics:

"A trip to the market guaranteed a dazzling range of traditional crafts repeated from one generation to the next without ongoing critical intervention and independent of religious function. The caves near my mother's village are full of prehistoric rock drawings and paintings. My eyes took in all of this; my painting allowed me finally to process the seemingly dissonant visual information."

He was an artist always, but what that meant in terms of making a life as an artist was still developing. "The painter as an individual, however, without church or mosque affiliation, and sanctioned by civilians and government is a relatively new concept for us in Eritrea, forty years old at most. When I paint in my studio in New Haven, some five thousand miles away from home, I still find myself reacting to this reality. My normative experience is inescapably Eritrean. And as it turned out for me, I also have to respond and account for the stimuli and influencing forces that I find myself open or vulnerable to, because of my life here. So far I have been able to cull the various forces such as Be-Bop, Modern Jazz (especially Thelonious Monk and Charles Mingus), polyrhythms of the African diaspora, and the great many paintings that I spend time viewing in museums, when I can take time off. I am continually recontextualizing my normative experiences in early Eritrea, and one of those manifestations has been my work as a chef, where I have found myself integrating cross-cultures into dishes. I have become a conscious synchretizer. My cooking is how I make my living, but I have also been able to make a creative experience that in fact complements my painting philosophy."

In his work is also the influence of maps, topography, the African and European study of geography, and the African awareness of changing maps and externally-imposed borders that cause so much suffering and chaos.

Connected to his love of books and his insatiable curiosity of mind was his relationship to languages. He spoke seven living languages well—Tigrinya, Amharic, Italian, English, Arabic, German, and Spanish. He could say hello and thank you in literally dozens of other languages ("What could be more important to know in a language besides 'thank you'?" he used to say) and was teaching himself Mandarin Chinese and French. His language acquisition was an emblem of the politics of colonialism and exile. Eritrea was for some time an Italian colony; he received a beautiful early education from Italian nuns and that was the language of extensive book study for him. Amharic, also, was a colonial tongue for a long, fraught period. Spanish came from long years of restaurant work, communicating intimately with the people he worked with in his kitchens. But his relationship to language also said everything about his respect for others, his sense of all of us as connected global citizens, and his constant curiosity to learn and then amalgamate different ways of thinking and being in the world. He was an Esperantist, someone who understood profoundly that languages are epistemologies as well as human bridges.

Ficre also connected language to visual expression. "Storytelling comes naturally in Eastern Africa, where the mainstay of culture is orally transmitted from generation to generation," he wrote. "Many Eritreans are still illiterate, and the culture of visual communication is relegated to Coptic Orthodox church facades and interiors. Murals and mosaics of saints and angels abound. There is an equally strong presence of Islamic iconography on the exteriors and interiors of mosques. Concomitant to these two ancient presences in my growing up years in the capital city of Asmara were war-time, mural-sized portraits of Marx, Engels, Lenin, Stalin, and—depending if he was in favor—Chairman Mao, as well as the Ethiopian dictator Colonel Mengistu Haile Mariam."

Ficre dreamed of one day opening an arts school in a peaceful Eritrea. "Of the few painters that currently live and work in postwar Eritrea, most are relegated to didactic renderings of social/realist views of the painterly praxis, and inasmuch they have not done much to instigate critical participation from viewers by speaking for themselves, instead they keep speaking about a pre-supposed community with pre-supposed needs and solutions. In the light of such a backdrop my dream school will be about self-exploration and expression. I believe in it will be found great seeds for healing and peace."

Five

The next day is Friday. There is some bad news in the extended family, and Ficre and I have been talking about whether, when, and how to inform our children. Solo is soon to turn fourteen, and Simon is twelve. We speak with them after school at the kitchen table, where all important conversations happen. They cry to hear the sorrows of one of their beloveds, but we answer their questions together and then I drive them to basketball practice, and we have the kind of unguarded post-mortem talk we often have on substantial car drives. By the time we pull into the gym parking lot, the children's eyes are dry and they seem to understand all they need to. On the way home after practice, we talk instead of what was upon us: the surprise fiftieth-birthday party they have planned for their father, which would occur the next day.

On Saturday, the boys and I are buzzy with barely managed anticipation as we try to go about our business as usual while surreptitious emails and calls come in with last-minute details and snafus. My brother stopped at the bakery in Bridgeport to pick up the cake and found the bakery closed. A friend from New York is waiting at a café downtown until the coast is clear. It is supposed to storm, and a friend from Boston is not sure that she can make it on the road. Finally Ficre and the boys leave the house and he takes them to see *The Hunger Games.*

I scurry around tidying up. In a few hours, friends begin to arrive, decked out and giddy. Solo and Simon and I had secured a New Haven party treat, The Big Green Truck: a truck with a brick oven for making pizzas with a cavalcade of toppings, plus salad, and gelato, and espresso. The pizza-makers are in on the secret and so park the truck out of sight by the side of the house.

Solo texts from the road, *We are leaving downtown. We pulled out of the parking lot. We're on Whitney Avenue.* Everyone gathers in the library, rustling and giggling, until we hear Ficre's key in the door. Surprise! His face wide open with joy as he goes to each one of us, *You,* and *You,* and *You*! We laugh, we talk, we eat, and we dance. In the living room, he and Amy, who he calls his Italian sister, exchange long hard shoulder rubs as they often do; his face is perfect contentment, eyes closed, as she rubs the tension out of his shoulders. I later ask Amy how Ficre felt to her that night and she said, "He surrendered to my hands. I never felt someone so relaxed."

That night, he goes to sleep literally with a smile on his

face. I gently poke him, thinking he is awake and playing sleep to entertain me, or still falling asleep, reviewing the evening in his mind. But he is deeply, profoundly in what the Senegalese poet Leopold Sedar Senghor called, in his poem "To New York," "a deep, negro sleep."

My brother, Mark, his wife, Tracy, our niece and nephew Maya and Calvin, and my sister-friend Alondra are sleeping in the house with us. In the morning Ficre gets up first as usual for a Sunday, and I go to Alondra's bed and get in to chat, and then Mark comes and sits at the end of the bed and we go over all the wonderful details of the party. *"Fratello! Mangia questa!"* Mark said Ficre kept exclaiming, as each pizza came out of the oven: roasted red pepper and sweet sausage; fresh tomato, garlic, and basil; goat cheese, fig, and caramelized onion. The two loved speaking Italian together. I tell Mark and Alondra how he fell asleep with a smile on his face. They cannot get over it.

That evening, something urgent and sharp comes over Ficre: he has to leave the house, right away, he tells me. He has to buy a lottery ticket; he has a number, and a feeling. He is agitated, so certain is he his number is going to win, and win big. I tell him gently he is being a little silly and let's just have dinner but he jumps in the car, runs off, and comes back with what I later discover is a stack of lottery tickets. "I have to win it for you," he says. "I have to win the lottery for you."

The next day, Monday, he is still not quite himself, running something in circles in his head. I say, why don't we meet at home for lunch. *Mangia, mangia* is my solution to most infelicities. He never eats lunch in the studio; maybe he just needs something to eat, I think. When we meet he is still mired in his strange, edgy mood. I thump his chest and say, spit it out! He looks relieved. "I feel better," he says, and we eat our green salads with grilled chicken in the backyard, where it is cool and fresh. His head seems straight. We each go back to work.

When he comes home, he is tired but I urge him to continue with his plan to shop for fixings for his *sugo alla Bolognese* with which to prepare his ravishing lasagna, for Easter comes this Sunday. We are hosting the extended family, arriving from various points in our particular African diaspora: Nairobi, Kenya; Oakland, California; Aberdeen, Scotland; Geneva, Switzerland; Montpellier, France; London, England; Montclair, New Jersey; Washington, DC; and New York, New York.

This is what Ficre puts in his Bolognese:

Diced pancetta
Diced prosciutto cotto
Ground veal
Ground beef
Fresh marjoram
Carrots
Onions

Celery
Whole milk
No garlic
Tomato

He makes the sauce, leaves it to cool, and then freezes it. We both sleep quickly and put the strangeness of the day behind us.

The next day, Tuesday, I have to be at the University through the evening, showing Charles Burnett films to my students. One of them is *When It Rains*, a short I have always loved that I first saw with Ficre in Chicago in the early days of our relationship. It is a parable set in another point of the West African diaspora, Leimert Park, Los Angeles. An urban griot and community wise man comes to the aid of a woman who is behind on her rent. African drums are ambient throughout the film, and the solution to the woman's dilemma is ultimately to be found in an obscure jazz record of incalculable value. Ficre loved what he called the film's "Africanity." It shows an urban American village filled with Africanisms and offers faith in simple resolutions, acts of kindness, and the curative power of black art, in this case, jazz.

I come home late. The boys are asleep and Ficre is on the couch watching television, waiting for me, drowsy, but wanting to know everything that happened. I am exhausted but we enjoy remembering that beautiful film.

He has promised Solo a sleepover. He and the boys operate in close proximity and cherish each other's nearness. He and I kiss each other. He goes to Solo's trundle bed and I go to our bed, and we call out good night to each other down the hall. How beautiful, the way that children sleep so deeply and peacefully that their parents' voices do not wake them.

The whole family sleeps and the house is still.

The next morning Ficre wakes exhausted, but happy. "This is the most comfortable bed I have ever slept in!" he says.

Then sleep some more, I whisper, and delay leaving home, puttering, so we can be together.

He feels better when he wakes again. We drink our coffee and chat, as on a million mornings. He drives me to work. I've just heard about a poetry reading on campus from a book of new translations of the sacred poetry of the Kabbalah, but it is scheduled at the same time I'm supposed to pick the children up from school to take them to the orthodontist.

"You have to hear the sacred poetry of the Kabbalah!" Ficre says to me. "You are an artist, and you need it—*I* will take the children to the orthodontist!"

And so I say Yes. And Thank you.

I love you, I say.

I love you, he says.

Have a wonderful day, and *Ciao Ciao*, we say.

How many times have we parted and said those words?

Six

At four, I go to a reading and conversation on the sacred poetry of the Kabbalah between the poet and translator Peter Cole and the campus rabbi and resident wise man, James Ponet. The room is packed; the words resonate and sound to me oracular and true, though their meaning is mysterious.

> *Windows of worship*
> *Windows of beckoning*
> *Windows of weeping*
> *Windows of joy*
> *Windows of satiety*
> *Windows of hunger*
> *Windows of penury*
> *Windows of wealth*
> *Windows of peace*
> *Windows of war*

Windows of bearing
Windows of birth

And he saw—
Windows without number and end

The program runs long so I tiptoe out to get home as promised.

The late afternoon light blazes and sparkles. Earlier, I'd called Ficre to check in. He has remembered to pick up the salmon I plan to cook for dinner, with roasted potatoes and sautéed broccoli rabe. Months later, when I can bear to return to the fish market, our fishmonger will tell me that Ficre was his usual cheerful self that day, joking in Spanish with the guys in the back as Lance cut him an extra-nice piece of fish. Once a chef, always a chef, with special courtesies.

I walk down Edgehill Road to the house from the bus. From his bedroom window lookout spot, Simon sees me approach and comes running downstairs to the door. "Big Solo is not coming to Easter!" he calls out. "Sólome has the chicken pox!" News from the family in diaspora: an admired older cousin in Montpelier, France, will not join us for the holiday as planned because his three-year-old daughter is contagious. I go inside and call to my husband, as I have called so many times—hundreds of thousands of times?—with a smile in my voice, "Fiiii-kiii!" "I'll get him!" Simon sings. Later I will look at video made close to that day of the children watching the rapacious hawk, and hear the light tinkling bells in Simon's voice and think, he was so young that April.

And then Simon is screaming. I run downstairs and see Ficre slumped on the floor, the treadmill still running. There is a raw slash where skin has come off of his head. I think, the treadmill was set too fast; he fell and hit his head. Which he had. I think, he will have a horrible concussion. There is a small amount of yellow fluid pooled next to him. Strangely, I see no blood. Some months later, Solo comes home from school and says: I know what the yellow liquid was. It was plasma. Blood separates into red and yellow, plasma and protein, he tells me.

I tell Simon: *Leave, get the phone, get your brother, call 911, bring me the phone*, and I am alone with Ficre. His eyes face mine directly. He is so warm; he is the right temperature. One half of his face seems slack to me so I then think, he has had a stroke and that it is worse than a concussion, but he will recover. I never think of his heart.

Both children appear with the phone; there is no time to engage their panic. 9-1-1. I speak to the operator. I experience myself as perfectly calm, cool, and collected, but she says, "Let me speak to the child, ma'am. You need to calm down. Put the child on the phone."

I tell the children: *Go upstairs, wait for the ambulance, bring them down quickly when they come.*

I am alone again with Ficre. It is just the two of us. I speak to him, low and urgent and gentle. I hold him carefully and try to wake him with my words and touch. I breathe into his warm mouth. I don't try to lift him, lest his spine be injured. I am certain he can hear me.

A young woman comes down into my basement, someone I have never seen. "I'm an RN. I was walking by your house and saw your boys outside, and they told me what happened. Let me help." An angel. She takes over the CPR and also calls 911 again and answers their questions. I cannot hear her answers. She is there when the paramedics come. When they move me aside to take over, I look to her to see if I should let them, and she nods. She is my guide now. I go upstairs. My next-door neighbor Stephanie is in the foyer. I call my friend Tracey, who lives around the corner, tell her Ficre has to go to the hospital and I need her to stay with the children.

The paramedics tell me I should ride with them to the hospital, but in the front with the driver, as they need space to "work on him" in the back. I want my hands on his body, so he knows I am there. It's me, Elizabeth. It's Lizzy. But they insist I sit in the front.

We drive down Whitney Avenue in slow motion. "I should call someone, shouldn't I?" I say, to the driver, who is a woman. "Yes, you should call someone," she says. "I don't know who to call," I say. The kids are safe, my parents are hundreds of miles away, and I don't know what is happening.

The medics rush him into the emergency room, and the doctors usher me in the roomette where they work. I keep my hand on his calf the whole time. He is still warm. They cut off his clothes. As his body is exposed, a doctor in a turban closes the curtains.

They pump him and jump him and IV him. They keep doing it. "Anyone have any other ideas?" shouts the doctor, after they have tried and tried. And then he looks straight and deep into my eyes and says the words they say in the movies that are nonetheless the only words: *We did everything we could do for him*. Which I saw. Later on I will learn it was 6:54 p.m., Wednesday, April 4, 2012.

The penis, which is mine alone, lies sleeping on his thigh, nestled in its hair, the heart outside his body, and that is what I remember of his body, after the emergency room doctor met my eyes and made his pronouncement. Him, still him, still Ficre, still a him, the last trace of him. The penis with which he actually made the human beings who are our children, is sign and symbol and substance of what I have lost.

I lie atop him and cover his body with my body. After time that cannot be measured someone I do not know comes and puts her arms around my shoulders and gently, gently leads me off and away from Ficre.

My cell phone does not work inside; the emergency room is being renovated. I go outside under a scaffold.

"Can you please bring the children to the emergency room entrance to Yale-New Haven Hospital to see their father, right now," I say, to Tracey, in a tone that says, *Ask no questions*, because I cannot lie to her.

And they come, and I am waiting for them at the entrance, and I tell them that Daddy is dead.

Seven

Then it is Solomon, Simon, and me. *Where is Daddy*, they ask. We go to a room to see his body—not to see him, to see his body, for when we go in, it is his body but not him, in a hospital gown, under covers. We touch and hug and weep over the body that no longer houses him. It is somehow not frightening to see this body. In these moments it still belongs to us. The body is no longer warm. Our wails are one wail. We know when we want to leave the room.

I reach my brother by telephone. He doesn't understand what I am saying but then he understands enough to say he is getting in the car in New Jersey and driving to Connecticut. Everyone in the emergency room is crying as I make that call, the boys my sentries.

Tracey has called Alondra in New York, who is coming, and she and Mark talk to each other from their cars as they both roar up the highway.

Tracey has called Emilie, who is a reverend, and I have called Lisa, my therapist. They are at the house when we return. Tracey has brought lavender tea. The tomato sauce she began to make for when we came home with Ficre—something practical, something to do with her hands—is in a pot on the stove, reduced to sticky sweetness.

Over and over I dial 202-544-8223, my parents' phone number for over forty years, but they are out late for dinner in Washington, DC. Finally I reach them. He is their son, and he is dead.

I call his eldest sibling, Tadu, who has just arrived in New York en route to the planned extended Easter celebration. I tell her plainly, Ficre has died, and then I tell her daughter, our niece, to be sure it is understood across our language barrier, and because it makes no sense and needs to be repeated to be true.

I somehow get the boys to bed, together. I fall into a black sleep without images.

Eight

Henry Ford believed the soul of a person is located in their last breath and so captured the last breath of his best friend Thomas Edison in a test tube and kept it evermore. It is on display at the Henry Ford Museum outside Detroit, like Galileo's finger in the church of Santa Croce, but Edison's last breath is an invisible relic.

Ficre breathed his last breath into me when I opened his mouth and breathed everything I had into him. He felt like a living person then. I am certain his soul was there. And then in the ambulance, riding the long ride down to the hospital, even as they worked and worked, the first icy wind blew into me: he was going, or gone.

"I need to call somebody don't I?" I asked the ambulance driver, a woman.

"Yes you do," she said.

Nine

Black men die more catastrophically, across class, than anybody else in America.

Toni Morrison: "Not a house in the country ain't packed to its rafters with some dead negro's grief."

He was an African man, an Eritrean man, and an African American man. He was a black man. He was not the descendant of slaves. He literally walked across his country through killing fields to escape, when he was sixteen years old. He walked into the dust of Khartoum. He was a refugee in Sudan, in Italy, in Germany, and in the United States, where he would end up living in New Haven, Connecticut, for far longer than he had ever lived anywhere. He washed dishes in Italy, attended school before he knew a word of the language in a Germany so racially hostile it almost broke him. He went years without seeing his parents. His parents and his community built him to survive. But it was not without price.

His big heart burst. The autopsy later tells us his arteries were blocked nearly completely, despite the fact that he was slim and energetic and ate yogurt and blueberries and flax-seed, despite the fact that he passed stress tests with flying colors. I learn that severe heart disease is first discovered in one of five sufferers when they drop dead. He could never quit smoking, though he tried and tried, over and over and over. Heart disease is the leading cause of death in the United States.

He was probably dead before he hit the ground, the emergency room doctor and the coroner and a cardiologist I later speak with tell me. That is why there was no blood on the floor, despite his head wound and the scalp's vascular-ity. He might have felt strange, the doctors told me, before what they call "the cardiac event," but not for more than a flash. One tells me he is certain Ficre saw my face as he died. We are meant to take comfort in this knowledge, if knowledge it is.

Ten

Because he was eminently strong of body and spirit, he went to the grocery store despite fatigue and bought supplies to make the Easter Bolognese. It was a busy week ahead and Monday was the night to shop and prep. I pushed him like an Italian wife as I always did: *vai, vai, vai*, and so he went to the store in preparation for his sauce, and started the cooking.

His last night on earth, I was out of the house, showing films to my students for class. Who could have known, but still, I look back and wish I had known and that we could have stayed up all night together, entwined, saying every single thing to each other and weeping. Like a man waiting for his execution, I think: a maudlin thought, but my fervent, despairing current wish is that we had every single moment, that I could have braved the countdown with him, that we could have walked the gangplank together.

But where would the children have been during this anguished, operatic exit? I could never allow that particular howling agony to touch them. For them I prefer no clue, no lead-up, no mortal dread.

Bill T. Jones choreographed and performed a dance called "Last Night on Earth" that emerged from his loss of his partner, Arnie Zane, to AIDS, and the ravaging of his community by the HIV virus. In the dance, he speaks from the stage to the audience, asking them sharp, direct questions: "What time is it? Can you at this moment look in the mirror and be all right with it?...Are you doing what you want to do *right*? Have you located your passion as if this was your last night on earth?" He gave his memoir that urgent, encompassing name.

His last night on earth, Ficre waited up for me. Tell me everything, he said. Now I was the one who went out into the world and came back with an armful of flowers, a cabinet of curiosities. He had had too much of the world; he loved hearth above all else. The best and worst of the world were all in his head. He put it on canvas and gave it to us. Because going out into the world can make you tired I couldn't always share every little thing and now I wish I'd poured a glass of wine and sat with him for hours on the red sofa and told stories like he did, all generosity, Frederick the mouse of Leo Lionni's classic children's book, offering his mouse community the sunlight of stories to get them through the long, dark winter. But it was very late after my extended workday, and I could not.

Monday he was deeply fatigued. Monday his mood was

peculiar and I tried to snap him out of it. He came home for lunch and felt better; he said so, in his sweet, sunny text messages: *Thank you for lunch*, and *The salad was good!*

His body was his same body, his same warmth and weight and smell.

If I go back to that late afternoon, I walked down the sparkling block and as I came up to the house, the boy came running to greet me. I can freeze the moment before we knew, before Simon ran through the basement door and found his father on the floor.

We three found him there on the floor. The big boy named for the wise king knew his father was dead. It never occurred to me he could be dead. The younger boy's thoughts were all magic, *If I had gone to check him*, Simon said, and *They'll bring him back.*

I breathed into his mouth. He was supple. The 911 operator asked if my husband was breathing and I could not say. The air around him was warm and vaporous. How many times that day and in following days and weeks and months did I say "my husband." My husband died unexpectedly. I just lost my husband. Lost implies we are looking, he might be found.

I lost my husband. Where is he? I often wonder. As I set out on some small adventure, some new place, somewhere he does not know, I think, I must call him, think, I must tell him, think, *What he would think?* Think what he thinks. Know what he thinks.

When I held him in the basement, he was himself, Ficre.

When I held him in the hospital as they worked and cut off his clothes, he was himself.

When they cleaned his body and brought his body for us to say goodbye, he had left his body, though it still belonged to us.

His body was colder than it had been, though not ice-cold, nor stiff and hard. His spirit had clearly left as it had not left when we found him on the basement floor and I knew that he could hear us.

Now I know for sure the soul is an evanescent thing and the body is its temporary container, because I saw it. I saw the body with the soul in it, I saw the body with the soul leaving, and I saw the body with the soul gone.

Eleven

The story begins in 1962, where two women in cotton lawn maternity shifts approach the end of their pregnancies, one in Asmara, Eritrea, one in Harlem, USA. The low-hanging moon of impending childbirth governs their days. The ones we may come to love have been born by the time we start longing for them, and so my beloved and I came onto this earth in March and in May of 1962, halfway around the world from each other. Then in 1996 we came together, one family who arrived in America as Eritrean refugees who had never been slaves, the other who landed one hundred, and two hundred, and three hundred years ago, slaves and free, from Europe, Africa, and the Caribbean.

Every beautiful day we lived, every single beautiful day.

II

HONEYCOMB

One

You tell the story.

No, you tell the story—

I had just recovered from a rather significant romantic mis-step and fled from Chicago to New Haven, to Yale, at the invitation of my director friend Leah, to write a play. I hoped new work would heal me.

A friend took me to see Reggie-the-Psychic-of-Brooklyn-New-York.

You better get yourself together, girl, Reggie said, because your man is on his way and you can't stop this love from coming.

This is no regular Negro, Reggie said. He's from some-place tiny that no one's ever heard of. I see you in a kitchen, picking up a conversation where you left off, even though you just met each other.

He's a painter, said Reggie. The paintings are big, and the colors look like sunset, like the American Southwest. I want one!

And here comes the baby! Reggie said. It's a boy, and he's coming sooner than you think.

And by the way, you want to be a playwright? Guess who you're going to meet tomorrow? Mister George C. Wolfe.

Pish-tosh, I thought, and then went on about my business. Reggie-the-Psychic. Hmph.

A few weeks later, I was sitting in a café in New Haven, drinking my orange pineapple smoothie and minding my own business.

I was to meet an old, old friend. Strangely, she never arrived.

Excuse me, he said, like so many songs go. I looked up from my book.

And thus we proceeded to talk.

I loved that she was an artist. I loved that she was a teacher. I loved that she had short hair.

A torque inside my stomach, the science of love.

I was headed back to Chicago that week and so wrote down for him, 517 West Roscoe Street, Chicago, Illinois, 60615, and then, last minute, my local telephone number for the next few days.

The phone was ringing when I went back to my campus apartment: *Would you like to come by for coffee tomorrow?*

And I said yes.

And he said, *Call me when you set out walking, and I will wait for you.*

There he stood on the corner of George and State Streets, waiting for me, smiling.

I went for coffee and I never left.

And did I remember to say? The day after speaking to Reggie, I met the great George C. Wolfe, at the theater in New Haven, totally by chance.

Two

When we first became lovers, we entered a three-day, three-night vortex. Night One I slept Senghor's "deep negro sleep" for the first time ever, lifelong insomniac no more. Night Two I burned with high fever and dreamed of my grandmother and a cherry tree, the only fruit she ever ate to excess. The next morning, Ficre gave me small sips of cold black currant juice and rosehip tea to make me well. Night Three my fever broke and so did my menses, more blood than I had ever let in my life, all over the bed, a trail across the room, the bathroom floor and in the tub. He cleaned it up; I did not feel abashed. Then he had to go to Washington, where there was to be an exhibition of photographs of Eritrea that he took during the long war and just after independence. He packed a small grip in thirty seconds and stepped lightly out the door. The last thing he put in the bag was my first book of poems. We left the loft together and off he zoomed down I-95 in his sister's borrowed Honda Accord.

He returned to New Haven five days later with a present for me: a honey-drenched honeycomb, from Luray Caverns. Its structure was ancient and iconic. *Did you know that honey was found in King Tutankhamen's tomb and is still edible?* he said. *And that honey was found in sealed jars in Pompeii?* We marveled at the honeycomb's simple construction and deceptive strength, and held it up to behold its incomparable gold. We looked all around us through the honey's gold light. Then we ate of it.

Three

We courted over six weeks in the summer of 1996. At the end of the first week, we decided to marry but told no one. *They'll think we're crazy!* we'd say. *It's our secret.* We were certain.

We ate little, drank sweet *cafecitos*, and listened to Ahmad Jamal, Betty Carter, Abbey Lincoln, Randy Weston, and Don Pullen, geniuses of the African diaspora we both celebrated. We wrote dozens of haikus back and forth in a shared notebook and he nicknamed himself "Basho in Africa." Basho wrote in the seventeenth century in Japan's Edo period and was thought to be the greatest practitioner of haiku, but he is even more renowned for leading others in renku, a collaborative, linked-verse poetry. No one had ever asked me to write poems together.

How I researched tiny Eritrea when I first met him! How I practiced saying his name correctly—FEE-kray Geb-reh-YESS-oos, playing his first answering machine message back over and over again to get it right. How I opened myself to learning this brand-new person from a brand-new, fascinating place. I came from the pig people and he came from the cow and the sheep people. Some of my people were midland slaves who made something from nothing and Massa's leavings. Some of my people were fancy and free. He came from forever-free Christian Coptic highlanders who alternate seasons of harvest bounty and Lenten veganism. That was the interesting idea of us: East and West Africa married, descendant of slaves who survived, descendants of free people of color, descendants of freedom fighters never enslaved, the strongest of all to be conjoined in our children. Sometimes we talked about this. But mostly we just talked, the deepest thoughts, the sweetest thoughts, the questions we had waited to ask forever. He was a bottomless boat and the boat that would always hold me.

His teeth were straight, white, and bright without benefit of American orthodonture. In photographs he disdained "cheesing" and set his lips firmly closed, but his smile was quick and shone full sunshine. He shaved his head on account of his receding hairline, and surely no one ever looked more beautiful bald—brown like a chestnut, clear brown, like topaz or buckwheat honey ("Did you know that buckwheat is neither grass nor wheat and is closely related to rhubarb?" I can hear him say). He was of medium build and trim, though he tended towards a wee bit extra around the middle that I found lovely. His fitness was that of a man who worked on his feet and could do things. He was nimble and physically intelligent. He hoisted large objects and moved them, climbed up on ladders, crawled behind and under furniture, jerry-rigged solutions to household problems. Later, when we had a home together, he would often work in the garden all day in hot sun; he paced himself and never seemed to tire. "You got yourself an African ox, baby," he'd say to me, as he pushed a wheelbarrow full of rocky dirt he'd dug to clear a patch for growing.

Nothing was out of place or excessive about him. He looked like one of several variations on an Abyssinian "type," which is to say large, wide-set eyes, broad, smooth forehead, a particular luminosity to his brown color, a carved nose. But he was, of course, only himself. His voice lilted across a pentatonic scale. "How are you?" D-sharp, C, G-sharp. There was chocolate in his voice, a depth, a bottom.

In this still life I have forgotten to say, he was beautiful, and utterly without vanity.

His work was in kitchens and in painting studios, so his everyday attire was T-shirts, jeans, and sneakers. He stood long hours and tried many different kinds of footwear but always came back to sneakers. Later after we were together, when I traveled to give readings and talks, I would bring him back the most unusual T-shirts I could find, which he loved for his daily uniform: La Brea Tar Pits; University of

Transylvania soccer team; Watts Towers Community Arts Center; Stax; Matthew Henson's brown face framed by a fur-lined parka. His studio was never adequately heated nor cooled so when painting he would add on another shirt, a sweater, and his beloved grass-green fleece vest, often along with a bright wool scarf and a knit cap, to keep the heat in. When we went out on occasions, he wore vibrantly colored button-down shirts with his jeans, guayaberas or dashikis in the summer. Upon meeting him, one new friend commented, "Ooh, I love a man who isn't afraid of a pop of color." "Pop of color" became a phrase we loved to repeat, and certainly no man ever looked finer in hot pink.

We talked all day and all night for six weeks straight. He told me everything about life in Eritrea in his family's compound, describing his father with children climbing all over him, laughing; his mother carefully choosing spices, or thread colors for embroidery, or paint colors for their walls, and letting him jostle her elbow so more clarified butter would go into the stew; he and his siblings washing the feet of the nuns who came by their house on Easter pilgrimage; the censers swinging through the Coptic church dispersing frankincense smoke; the big-eyed icons in stained glass, and the booming African drums making no mistake that this ancient Christianity was African; his reading the Italian newspapers aloud to his father; the Italian deco buildings of downtown Asmara, which remain the finest examples of that architectural style in the world; the best gelato ever accompanying his beloved *cinema*—pronounced in Italian—in the deco movie theater; his reverent love of the classroom and his teachers, who cherished him; the day his teacher read his essay aloud, and said, "Bambini, this one among you shall become a great writer"; his school chained shut the very next day as the Red Terror accelerated; neighborhood friends disappeared without explanation; the angles of growing fear and life-or-death protection.

During part of our six-week New Haven courtship, three of his young nieces Amal, Bana, and Aden visited from Nairobi and northern Virginia. We drove them to Cape Cod and pretended they were our children—for they were—and they danced magic spells around us, blessing our union. He and I would drive into New York late at night after he finished his shifts at the restaurant, and on slow days. He'd take me to the places that were most important to him when he lived in New York as an impassioned activist, also beginning to paint at his uptown kitchen table. We visited the Art Students League, Bob Blackburn's printmaking workshop, and a performance of the Mingus Big Band. He loved to listen to "Fables of Faubus" over and over again, its oompah-loompah belying the sharp social commentary on the crumbling order of deep Jim Crow. We ate Italian food at a sidewalk café in the neighborhood he charmingly called "the" Soho. We walked to Veniero's pastry shop in the East Village for millefoglie and espresso. Then we drove home to New Haven and here is one of dozens of small ways I knew I had met my love: me, the inveterate backseat driver began to fall asleep, safe with him at the wheel. I let go. It was perfectly quiet inside the car. And then I woke to a sentence he spoke, his rich, deep voice catching with emotion. "Lizzy," he said, "you have land in Africa."

Four

I returned to Chicago to my job, but we had pledged our troth. All we had to do was get through the teaching year and then I would move and we would be together. He had not yet met my parents but my father said, *I know you and see how you are now that you are with him, so I know this man is right.* He came to visit in Chicago and met my chosen family there. He cooked a feast for my people and teenaged children, and Mona and Bernardine—the groups' elder sisters to me—telephoned my parents on the spot and had a very serious conversation with them: *Yes, they'd met the man. This is why he is good. This is how he loves her.* How did my life become so African? I whispered to Ficre with a smile, as we watched the modern-day village elders bless our union. Soon after we went to Washington to my parents, and after talking with him about history for hours after breakfast, my mother pronounced, "I have known him all my life."

He spoke to me often about the wide skies he grew up

beneath in Eritrea, and the red rocks in the highlands. It sounded like what I had heard about the American Southwest, so I planned a trip for us. We went to Albuquerque, and Santa Fe, drove the high road to Taos, ate fresh tortillas and saw the blood-stained walls of the church of the penitents, followed a black hawk down a river for dozens of miles, and sat on boulders in the cool fresh air, tilting our faces to the impossibly bright sunshine, soaking in its pure energy. Everywhere we went, fleece from cottonwood trees swirled around us, like a conjurer's transformative wind. We lived out of time for two weeks.

The advent of the Hale-Bopp comet was imminent. We felt we were chasing it, or it was chasing us. In Ojo Caliente, a hot spring in northern New Mexico, we watched stars streak across the sky, the moon evaporate into eclipse, all gone save a bright white sliver and red Mars. We watched from a lithium spring, arsenic bath, iron tub. Salty water steamed from the ground. In the lounge we watched our first TV in days and saw that people from a strange cult called Heaven's Gate interpreted in the same comet a doomsday directive and so ate poison in applesauce, drank vodka, and died. They believed they were going to the spaceship. When we kissed, we tasted minerals on each other's lips. We ate peach pie on the wrap-around porch. We saw a total lunar eclipse in Sedona. Somewhere there is a picture of us that we asked a stranger to take as we watched the sunset from a hillside in a crowd of hundreds, and everyone clapped when the burning orb dropped out of view. In Havasupai, we hiked the ten miles down to the reservation. You could hear the waterfall before you saw it. Brilliant-colored wildflowers abounded. You could also hear reggae; the gospel of Bob Marley played everywhere. The Indians respected Ficre because he was an African, an ancient man. We ate what seemed to be there: hot dogs and ketchup and fry-bread and M&M's.

We drove—he drove—2,000 miles. He prided himself on being a road warrior. One night we drove across an infinite field under the stars and heard Navajo on the radio, and then someone speaking to Jesus, and then, sounds from the spaceship. I found a bit that Ficre wrote about that trip, and for some reason, it was in Spanish. It begins, "*Eramos dos.*" We were two, the last people left on earth.

Five

He called his mother in faraway Asmara to tell her we were marrying. I got on the phone, having learned my *"selam"*— "hello"—and *"Kemay aleka"*—"how are you," if speaking to a woman—and though we did not share a language, I felt her gladness at her beloved son's happiness in the tones of our talk. He hung up the phone and said, "I miss my mother," and wept for the first time in my presence. This was life in diaspora.

We waited a year impatiently until the end of my teaching quarter at the University of Chicago and then he drove out to the city of big shoulders I had come to love so well, loaded up the car, and took me to New Haven. That was June of 1997. August 16 we were married in Saint Barbara Greek Orthodox Church in Orange, Connecticut, the closest we could get in New Haven to the church of his childhood. Then I changed from my simple wedding gown into a traditional Eritrean dress and we danced in hundred-degree heat in his brother Gideon's New Haven backyard to Congolese rumba played by a pan-African band called Dominicanza. Our guests ate injera and stews. We danced the consecrating *guayla* under a canopy held aloft by our families, who each took turns coming under to bless us. Two of his older female relatives beat small oil drums. The men danced with ferocious grace in a circle together. My brother's two small children, Maya and Jonah, twirled from soul to soul. In the middle of it all I slipped away and went inside to lie down in an upstairs bedroom, my cheeks burning with our secret. The heat and the music came through the wide-open windows from outside. I fell into a profound sleep, my hand on the baby quickening within me. When I woke and rejoined the celebration, at the peak of the August New Haven humidity, a wild storm briefly broke and then, Dear Reader, there appeared a double rainbow, the first I had ever seen. Some of the Eritreans slept under the wedding tent in the backyard and even the next day, there was ululation as they awakened. Ficre and Elizabeth were married.

Six

The first mistake a non-Habesha wife makes is the teakettle. Eritrean spiced tea is a treat and a daily ritual. The kettle is filled with cardamom pods, cinnamon bark, gingerroot, and cloves, so that the water is always infused with the spices. The tea—in our case, strong Kenya tea, brought or sent by Ficre's sister who lives in Nairobi—is sometimes boiled loose-leafed in milk and then brought to the right level of intensity with the flavored water. Or a quick tea is made with the spiced water and a teabag, and lots of sugar and heated milk are added. Delicious either way, always proffered for company, which in the Habesha household, is never-ending. Habesha: a word I learned and loved, meaning Eritrean and Ethiopian people. Some say Queen Hatshepsut in 1460 BC first used a version of the term to mean a foreign people from the incense-producing regions. In contemporary use, it is an interesting term of self-identification because it refers to Ethiopians and Eritreans, despite the historically rooted enmity that lingers amongst some in both groups.

One day the new, non-Habesha housewife will fill and put on the kettle, bring it to the boil, and empty the water into a soup she is making, or accidentally use it to steam vegetables, or pour it over French-press coffee. She will shriek at the brackish brown water and sticks that rush out. Thereafter there will be two kettles on the stove, and she will always remember which is which.

Though tea is usually taken with milk and sugar for the Eritrean highlanders abroad, Ficre said his mother occasionally liked it with sugar and a slice of lime when she took tea with her friends in the afternoon, as she also liked papaya, with a slice of lime.

I close my eyes and see the color of papaya, of all melons, and the walls of the home he grew up in, and their delicate reprisal in his paintings.

Seven

"I find the nest and you feather the nest," he would say.
I called him from Munich, where I was on a poetry
junket right after our marriage, newly pregnant with
soon-to-be-Solomon, who seemed to us the first child born
on earth. "I found our apartment," he said, after I had
complained that though I loved his painting studio, it was
not a place for us to have a baby, with its exposed nail
heads on the floor, twenty-four-hour construction outside,
frequent fire-code violations, and mouse visitors. He found
a beautiful two-bedroom apartment with a proper dining
room—my heart's desire—and we moved in as soon as I
got back.

Months later, with the child to be born within weeks,
Ficre came home one night late from the restaurant and
told me he had something he had to show me, now. It was
raining, it was midnight, and I was a zeppelin, anticipating the falafel he would bring me after work and which
we would eat while watching *Frank's Place* and *Frasier* in

reruns. Come, come, come! he exhorted, against my pro-
testations. He held the umbrella for me as I waddled three
blocks down our street.

He stopped us in front of a house that was blazing with
light so that we could see two men inside on ladders, painting the walls. We walked around to the backyard.

"Look," Ficre whispered. The men saw us at the window
and, improbably, beckoned us in. Would you like to see
the house? they said. And walked us through, at midnight.
There was going to be an open house on Sunday, they told
us. The next morning, we called the broker and preempted
it, for Ficre had found our home.

As soon as the aptly named Solomon was born—
righteous little man who blazed into this world fist-first—
and I could stay on my feet, the family from both sides
gathered to help us move. The men swiftly and silently
loaded a U-Haul truck with our belongings, proud African oxen all. A collection of nieces and my parents walked
lamps and glasses and garment bags back and forth the few
blocks between the apartment and the house, and I carried
the baby pasha to his palace.

With milk crates as our tables and chairs, we fortified
ourselves with legendary New Haven pizza and set up our
home. Solomon's room gleamed with buffered light off the
hardwood floors. The cradle our carpenter friend Carlo had
made us was in the corner. Our eldest niece, Senayt, set
up the diaper pail with the fancy closure that neither Ficre

nor I could figure out. One of Ficre's sisters made ga'at, the dense barley porridge meant to saturate the mother with iron after childbirth and repair her uterus. It is presented in a mound with an indentation in the center, into which is poured hot, clarified butter spiced with berbere, then cooled with yogurt.

Life on Livingston was lovely. Annie Fischer lived next door. She was an extraordinary gardener whose plate-sized flowers were her glory. I overlooked her yard from the window in the room where I worked. In summer she had loud, boozy parties on the back porch and we would go to sleep smiling listening to her raucous laugh, her joy, the sound of tinkling ice in g-and-ts. She had old rusty tin signs in the yard and a bench for sitting and thinking. She used to come to the fence with flowers for us, calling *FIIII-KIIII*, to him in his backyard studio, just as he came to her so many mornings with cappuccino as he went into the backyard to have his first cigarette and inspect his organic plot.

A creamy magnolia soon bloomed outside the window on my side of the bed. I can see our bedroom closet, the 1950s sparkling tile shelf, our bureaus side by side, the slant roof area he painted a color called cyan, which he told me was made by mixing green and blue light and which as dye was first derived from cornflowers. He painted the nook in which the kitchen garbage stood, green, bright green, watermelon-rind green. We kept family pictures on the built-in shelves leading up the stairs, an ancestral procession marking the way from the public first floor to our sleeping quarters.

I listened to Ficre sing the delicate Tigrinya melodies of his childhood as he rocked Solo in his golden room in the chair my students and colleagues gave me. Soon I knew the melodies as well and would sing like a silver bell, inserting the baby's name and turning it every which way, mimicking the shared deep sounds of Ficre's childhood, the pentatonic scales of Solomon's father's language. And I sang the songs of my own childhood, and my mother's, some of which were from Tidewater Indians, some from Alabama Africans. *Keemo Kimo Dairy-o, me-I, me-yo.* I later look up the song and find that Nat King Cole sang a version of it, and he called it "the magic song." Did Nat King Cole remember it from his own forbearers? Or did my grandmother sing it to me because Nat King Cole recorded it in 1947? It is all romance; all that imprecise romance rains down on the head of the beloved baby.

Ficre held Solo up to the birds in the trees because he believed that Solo could understand them. "Listen, they are singing back to him! They understood him!" he whispered.

For nine years we lived at 45 Livingston Street in New Haven, Connecticut, the house where we made family. We had our children there and welcomed extended relatives there for holidays and long stays as they were scattered by war, politics, and health challenges. One Easter a play-uncle of mine from Baltimore joined the table. "Your life is just like a foreign film!" he said, all of us around the table, drinking red wine and eating and talking and laughing. Ficre home-roasted coffee; string-tied boxes of Italian pastry appeared and disappeared in puffs of powdered sugar. Having grown up with one sibling, the children of two only children, my brother and I were without blood uncles, aunts, or cousins. "Your father was meant to be an African elder with all these children around for him to preside over," my mother said. "We just didn't want to actually *have* all those children." That I would be at the center of a big, extended African family seemed somehow karmic balance, the inevitable chapter in this story.

Eight

"The days are long but the years are short," some say, about the early years of child rearing. I remember some days being almost gelid in their slowness when Solo was a baby. I had never experienced time so consciously. Collapsed on the bed with him in strong afternoon sunshine, holding him up to the light and watching the light inside of him, listening to his birdsong. Time moved as though through honey.

And then, so quickly, two babies, with the arrival of Simon Alexander Ghebreyesus just a year and five months after his brother. We decided together that Ficre would commute to New York in those days as there was a rare opportunity to start a second Caffé Adulis in the city with his younger brother. He said he'd give it one year. We were builders! We were ambitious! We could do anything! But oh—the babies would wake chirping to the garbage trucks at five those mornings when Ficre was away, and I would count the minutes until Lulu's cafe opened and I could make my way over with my two plump boys and steady myself for the day with her strong coffee and a split and toasted sesame panini, in the society of other babies and toddlers and parents. The night before my first return to university life to deliver a lecture, the boys were up all night frolicking, would not sleep. Ficre was working in New York. I called him on the phone at two in the morning and he sang to them over the wires until we all three fell asleep in our bed.

He called me Lizzy.

Time began to move quickly when he was back full time in New Haven. His mother and his aunties made sure that I knew that I was lucky because when he was a child he always loved his home and never strayed. He is man who has drunk his water, his mother would say, which is the best kind of man to marry: one who is experienced in the world, but who is sated, who has had enough, who needs no more than his wife and children and work and home. When he was a teenager he ran away to join the war—he wanted to be a freedom fighter, like his brother Kebede and so many others—and his mother went and brought him back. But that was another story, and another time. When I knew him, he had drunk his water.

Nine

When my mother-in-law was dying, she faced illness with tremendous equanimity. She did not want pain—and luckily, medicine could take care of that—but she was not afraid of dying. We never saw her flinch in its face. I had always been afraid of death, waking from nightmares of its imminence even in my childhood. Much to my surprise, I was able to be present and useful and near to her as death approached near. I was surprised to learn I could sit by the side of death. I was grateful to be able to help this great woman who by example showed me so much of what it meant to be a matriarch. By letting me near, she showed me I was much stronger than I'd known I was.

The last word we heard Zememesh Berhe say was "*bun*," which means coffee, in Tigrinya, and which stands for so much more that is encompassed in the Eritrean coffee ritual. Green coffee beans are roasted in a long-armed aluminum pot with the onomatopoeic name *menkeshkesh*, for the sounds the beans make when the person roasting shakes the pan gently, carefully watching for when the oils began to gleam and the beans to brown. Once the beans are roasted to the desired depth of flavor, the roaster takes the pan around the room, beginning with the eldest person present and going to each person, inviting them to fan the coffee smoke to smell it. We gave this job to Solo when he was just old enough to carry the hot pan. Then the beans are spread to cool on a straw mat called *mishrafat*, then ground and brewed three different times and served in tiny, handle-less china cups called *finjal*, almost always with sugar and sometimes with warmed milk. I learned to say "*tu'um*" for delicious. It is considered very rude to leave before "third coffee," for each stage comes with its own blessing and marks more space for communal chat. How I loved to watch Ficre perform this ritual, and then to see the pride with which our eldest son learned it from his father. Coffee ceremony was the most sacred home ritual there was.

My mother-in-law's last night on earth, a fox crossed our path in Branford, Connecticut, as we left the hospice. We knew somehow that it was her, as I now know the ravenous hawk came to take Ficre. Do I believe that? Yes, I do. Poetic logic is my logic. I do not believe she was a fox. But I believe the fox was a harbinger. I believe that it was a strange enough occurrence that it should be heeded. Zememesh Berhe, the quick, red fox, soon passed from this life to the next.

Ten

We had fifteen Christmases together. Almost fifteen years of marriage, sixteen years together, 1996 to 2012. We always said it felt like longer than it was. I would estimate at the end that we had a twenty-five-year marriage, and Ficre would agree. That long, that much struggle, that much jubilee. In our extended family, and family of friends, two cancers, two heart surgeries, one drug addiction, two mental hospitalizations, marriages, babies, funerals. Easters and Thanksgivings. Our friends' parents and one friend's son died; together we went bearing food and hot coffee. Together we went to the various places of worship in our best black clothes. Three houses, two cities. One job change, two closed businesses, one started business. Money went, money came. Several bad boyfriends of nieces, several good, three lovely husbands of nieces, one lovely wife of a nephew, six lovely babies. Four homes owned, three sold. Hemorrhoid surgery, dental surgery. No broken limbs. One political regime change, the end of one war, the start of another. An East African American U.S. president. Several refugees. Two U.S. naturalization swearings-in: two new citizenships.

Together we chose two day-cares, two nannies, fired one nanny in six days because at one and a half Solo said NO, stayed with the other for three years and wept when it was time for her to leave us, one nursery school, two elementary schools, one middle school, one high school. We planned fifteen Thanksgiving dinners, fifteen Easters, and at last, one Feast of the Seven Fishes. One Easter Ficre found a sheep farmer in Cheshire, Connecticut, and had a lamb slaughtered for his sister Tadu, for her *tsebhe*—the rich and spicy Eritrean meat stew—and her roast. We found where we could buy Italian Easter bread shaped in a cross with hard-boiled eggs baked in. *Buon Pascua*, he'd say, and so would I.

Three trips to Italy, where we had family and which was our ironic colonial demi-motherland, each time to different places: Rome, Venice, Florence, Amalfi, yes, but also Bari, Ceglie, Ferrarra, to see in-laws and friends. London, Scotland, Spain, Oakland, the diaspora of our family. Milan awaited, and *bella Toscana*, and Naples, once the crime settled down, and Sicilia; he wanted to smell the mint crushed underfoot. The Alhambra awaited, and the orange blossoms in Southern Spain in very early springtime.

In the years we were together I wrote four books of poems, two books of essays, two edited collections, and countless essays and talks. I taught hundreds of young people African American literature and poetry, directed a poetry center, and chaired an African American studies department. He made over eight hundred paintings, countless photographs and photo collages, and ran two restaurants. Of the plans that did not come through we wrote menus for other restaurants, plans for a downtown New Haven arts center, a school for the arts in Eritrea, a bed-and-breakfast on the Hudson River, a play based on the life of the magician Black Herman. Each of us made it possible for the other. We got something done. Each believed in the other unsurpassingly.

In all marriages there is struggle and ours was no different in that regard. But we always came to the other shore, dusted off, and said, There you are, my love.

Eleven

For years we spoke of preparing the Feast of the Seven Fishes. We talked to people who we knew had cooked their version of the feast. And so we finally did it, with Amy and Joanne and their children Benjamin and Marina, a family dear to us. Amy is a first-generation Italian American. She and Ficre spoke Italian to each other with gusto and joy. He sang to Marina a song that Amy remembered from her childhood, "Marina Marina," in his sweet voice that brought her to tears. "Marina, Marina," he sang, sweet bells. *"Mi sono innamorato di Marina / una ragazza mora ma carina."* Brown-haired, beautiful Marina, *"una ragazza mora."*

We prepared and indeed we feasted. Cold seafood salad was the only thing we purchased, from a Pugliese market in North Haven. I made *linguine con le vongole* and white bean and tuna bruschetta. Ficre seared a large diver scallop for each of us and placed it in a freshly made salsa in the shell. I fried flounder so crisp it curled; Ficre never fried—"that's what your people do," he'd say, and we'd laugh. He ate that yummy fish. Anchovies in Caesar salad counted, we figured. And the final fish was Ficre's tuna, peppered, seared, and placed in strips on a bed of arugula and chopped tomatoes and a thin ribbon of balsamic vinegar reduction.

Each course left us silent with rapture. The children all said it was the best Christmas ever. Everyone loved their gifts. Amy gave Ficre fine Italian-made socks in salmon, cantaloupe, and shamrock green, which he preserved in the box they came in, waiting for the right occasion.

Twelve

Ficre thought Solo and Simon each should have a special ritual for his thirteenth birthday, and so he asked them to imagine a journey they'd like the family to take with them. "I want to take the Orient Express from Paris to Istanbul!" said Simon the younger, and so that trip became part of the family anticipatory fantasy, despite the fact that we weren't even sure if the Orient Express still ran. After characteristic deliberation, Solo declared that he wanted us to drive cross-country.

We planned and planned for two years leading up to the summer of 2011, when Solo would turn thirteen. We worked and organized to take six weeks. And then, the June day came.

We rented a car, the Crown Vic, in Stamford, our mighty chariot for the journey. Single-pump gas stations in the South. Peaches. Every civil rights stop we could make. The Edmund Pettus Bridge; Sixteenth Street Baptist Church; the Lorraine Motel. George Washington Carver's preserved laboratory at Tuskegee Institute. My grandparents' birthplaces in Alabama;

my great-grandparents' gravestones there. The Navajo rodeo, Navajo anthem, Navajo flag, Navajo-land. The Navajo speeding ticket, which Ficre prized. We were too tired to stop at the Grand Canyon. The rainstorm in Mississippi as we drove to Memphis, where it rained horizontally and Ficre piloted us through. To our children's vast amusement, we both rode the water slide at the Broadmoor in Colorado, the fancy hotel where I insisted we stay so that I could "revitalize" myself.

I had a gig in beloved Chicago, and the boys went to a White Sox game on the El while I read my poems.

We met friends. Kevin made us eat bacon dipped in peanut butter and Jennifer, fried pickles.

The Watts Towers, my holy place.

It was too hot to hike in Joshua Tree National Park, too hot to sleep in Palm Springs.

Hilarious Vegas, where we had lunch with a play-uncle of mine who is a singer there, and he met my children for the first time.

I argued like a grifter for a better hotel room in Santa Monica and we lived in the very lap of luxury.

The day in Santa Monica when we rented bikes and rode to Venice Beach in the sunshine. We zoomed on our separate bikes together, stopped to go to an actual freak show where a bearded woman greeted us at the door, and a man lay down on a bed of broken glass, and the children were growing and happy and free and we were using our bodies, and the ocean was beside us, and later we would eat fish tacos, and watch people dance to disco music and roller-skate, and then a drumming circle of about a hundred played on the beach as the sun set. This was the most perfect four hours of happiness in my life.

Our culminating stop was Oakland, where we visited his eldest sister. When we got there, the idyll halted when we learned that she had an advanced cancer. Ficre and I took it on like we always did, finding the very best doctors, contacting NIH about experimental protocols, reading and deciphering pathology reports, talking with her children. That was what we did in the family.

In many cultures and religions they warn you about looking too hard at one thing, because something can happen behind your back. West Indians give their children nicknames so the angel of death will not find them; he only knows to look for them by their proper names. When Solo was born, an Egyptian friend gave us an evil eye and told us to pin it into his stroller blankets, and indeed, I was glad it was there when people reached in to touch the exquisite child. We got another evil eye, and put it at the front of the house, along with a Chinese red rooster in the kitchen, everything but a mezuzah. I believe in all the charms and superstitions I did not grow up with, the beautiful objects that keep a family safe.

We light candles for Tadu with one hand and call NIH with the other. She makes plans to travel to Lourdes. Miraculously, her cancer will retreat. No one can understand it.

III

"The Edges of Me in the Hands of My Wife"

One

There you are, out the back bedroom window in early morning light, bundled in your red hat with the gold piping, your grass-green fleece vest, a fuzzy scarf. You are smoking and drinking coffee, perambulating the side yard, walking, clearly thinking. You would sometimes set up camp in the gazebo on nice days with the newspaper and coffee and cigarettes, surveying the yard and our home, guarding the roost. For a time you liked an old wicker table and chair stationed on the side by your vegetable garden, where you could watch the main street and all who drove or walked there. But mostly you liked standing and thinking by the side door of the house, never too far.

I tap on the window and wave. Your smile breaks open in return as you wave up; such pure happiness and light. I am here in the house, you are there through the window, and we are together: *Contigo en la distancia*, you like to say, and sign your notes, to me.

Two

Two days after the funeral it was Easter, and Cindy drove down from Boston with all the fixings for Easter dinner, including a ham. We have to have Easter, she said. I watched her slim fingers peeling potatoes and dicing white onion at the kitchen table with my mother. This is how we do.

A few weeks later, Robin brings another whole ham wrapped up in heavy-duty aluminum foil in a roller bag on Metro North. When she arrives, she starts the oven and studs the ham with cloves and yes, pineapple rings. We sit and talk quietly as the house begins to smell like a million Negro homes across the miles and the years. Eat something, baby, she said. Some ham on a homemade cloverleaf roll. Please, honey, eat just a bit.

Ficre loved the cri de coeur from August Wilson's play *Two Trains Running*: "I want my ham!" He called those plays so African, the ways Wilson's communities absorb their eccentrics and make space for them, without explanation.

Once on a trip to St. Croix in the Virgin Islands, we went to visit an artist friend of my parents' who made tie-dyed fabric and dresses. We sat in her atelier on a Saturday afternoon as folks wandered in and out, soliloquized, and left. The preacher, the hustler, the wino, the diva, all came in without announcement, said their piece, and exited stage right. It's so African! said Ficre, in love with the quotidian theater. It's like Africa, and it's like an August Wilson play!

Do you see why I miss him? I call out, to no one. Will I remember everything? What am I meant to keep?

Three

"It's the shock, not the grief, baby," my hairdresser says, as he runs his hands over and through my newly coarse, wildly gray hair.

Four

Three times a week at bedtime I'd put my tongue out like a kitten and he'd place a single baby aspirin on it. We entered middle age together. Baby aspirin are supposed to prevent heart attacks.

Five

I dream my house has no exterior walls, only the walls between rooms. The roof is afloat. I am on the first floor, open to the elements. An icy wind is blowing. I have no shawl.

I open my eyes and turn to his side of the bed. For the first time I begin to take the actual, physical measure of what I alone have lost. I picture and trace with my index finger his warm chestnut scalp, its furrows, and the seam down the center of his bald brown head. I feel the exact heft of him, his length lying next to me, the small bit of stomach that my hand held when I curled around him, my latch to his body.

I outline his fine nose. I feel the precise bristle of his mustache; note the exact proportion of black hairs to gray, their coil and spring. I look into his eyes, and the blue-gray ring around their brown irises: cholesterol, it turns out, creates that ring. But it is beautiful. I touch his plum-colored, pillowy lips. I see his face as he sleeps. Only I know how his face looks when he is deeply sleeping.

Sometimes in the morning as he finished a dream he would speak in Tigrinya as he began to wake. The boys have seen this when they would come to kiss him in the morning. How we loved when it happened! We'd stay very quiet in hopes the language would continue. He'd soon open his eyes, find us close to his face, and laugh a slurry, sleepy, awakening laugh.

I look for him now in the robust trees and in the custard-yellow magnolia he planted for me that actually bears my name, "Magnolia acuminata Elizabeth." I look for him in the peonies as big as a baby's head that he put in the ground for me, look to the small wicker table in the garden where he sat, drank coffee, and read the newspaper. It is fitting that the last photograph we have of him is in his garden. Look at his eyes in that picture, the kindest eyes anyone has ever seen. They still look out from amongst the green vines in his garden, his fagioli and figs. Fichi d'india, prickly pear fruit: I remember when we first saw, and then ate them, in southern Italy at our nephew-in-law Vito's parents' home in Ceglie, and we laughed because we called Ficre "Fiki" and now the Italian language rendered him a prickly pear, with the sweetest fruit inside.

Six

Ficre is not here to tell me what kind of trees my parents are, but I know they are mighty trees. They do not yield to the wind; they go straight up, unbending. Redwood seems too regionally imprecise; we are definitely not westerners. I think of my parents as having many colors ranging from the new greens of spring to autumn golds. But they have the constancy of perennials. All shelter and trunk to lean on, my parents stand like trees and survey everything. I am always their child, and yet, it is not as when I was a child, because I am also mother to Solomon and Simon, for whom I must be a tree. Ficre planted trees for me that were lush and romantic: magnolia, Japanese maple, for those were the years of amorous love and its fulsome expressions which sustain us through the winter months of marriage.

Now I need to be, like my parents, the one-hundred-year-old oak in our backyard that lives even after hammocks and tire swings have been nailed in and taken down and after the southern Connecticut tornado of 1989 destroyed wide swaths of Hamden as the wind tore down the streets uprooting trees. Our one-hundred-year-old tree stood, as my parents stand, as they saw elders stand, as ancestors stood.

During the funeral and the months after they come back and forth from Washington. My mother roasts chickens and sets tables and my father gets in the car and buys groceries and non-essential electronic appliances. Never once do they allow their grief to supersede even a corner of our home. And yet, it comes over me like another enormous dark cloud: they have lost a son. They have lost a son. They do not cry in front of me until I am much, much stronger. Then, it is first my father who weeps.

To be a parent is to be terra firma, to stand, is to be planted in the earth.

Ficre was supposed to be an elder, but his days were not long.

Seven

In Lucille Clifton's poems, the living and the dead speak across the veil. Over the years I have read those poems over and over, especially this one:

The death of fred clifton
11/10/84
Age 49

i seemed to be drawn
to the center of myself
leaving the edges of me
in the hands of my wife
and I saw with the most amazing
clarity
so that I had not eyes but
sight,
and, rising and turning,
through my skin,
there was all around not the

shapes of things
but oh, at last, the things
themselves.

Was that what dying was like, a drawing into essence, a concentrated drop that would then evaporate off the earth? "I seemed to be drawn," Clifton writes, in the voice of her dead husband; he cannot be sure of what is happening. But the dead husband speaks from solid ground when he states in the poem that he is "leaving the edges of me/in the hands of my wife." We grasp at the tattered edges and don't let go. What we clutch is a rent garment. But it is ours, and what is left, now.

The poem yields more as Fred Clifton moves closer to true knowing, as he sees with "the most amazing/clarity." Death itself is like a snake shedding its skin. Fred Clifton describes "rising and turning/through [his] skin." A new self reveals itself when the old carapace has shed and died, as though we live in exoskeletons with something truer underneath.

Death comes with a gift in the poem; our loved ones tell us here that what we see with our eyes is different from what we know: "The things/themselves." "Oh, at last" is the moment of exaltation in the poem. Lamentation and exaltation are simultaneous here.

I am a widow. I am Ficre's widow, clutching at his edges. I cannot hold on to the garment. I cannot imagine what sight awaits me.

Eight

He who believed in the lottery.

He who did not leave a large carbon footprint.

He who never met a child he didn't enchant.

He who loved to wear the color pink.

He whose children made him laugh until he cried.

He who never told a lie.

He who majored in physics, who knew the laws of the universe.

He who wanted to win the lottery for me.

Nine

May ninth, one month and five days after he died, he almost comes back. The children and I amble in the garden, enjoying his domain. The boys take turns standing on his top-of-the-world grassy mount. Perhaps four feet at its tallest point, Ficre piled and packed the dirt left from furrowing the garden's rows. From his mount, he worked and surveyed.

It begins to lightly rain and the boys scurry inside. I can see Ficre plainly atop his hillock. *Come on!* I say to him from the side door, gesturing towards the house. *Come in from the rain.* He stays where he stands, his eyes an infinity of sadness. *Please, please, come in*, I implore. He is outside and we would be inside, not forever but for a long, long time.

I muffle my cries so the children will not hear me, but months later, they will say, Mommy, we always used to hear you weeping in the garden.

The next morning I return to bed in a quiet house after

the children leave. I wail like an animal and then I sleep, and Ficre comes right to the edge of my dreams, no narrative, just presence, like a mother by her fevered child's sickbed. I think, I will keep mornings free for the rest of my life so I can go back to bed and hope to meet him there. He will take my hand and lead me somewhere. He is on the edge of sleep, and all I have to do is go there to be with him. I will go back to sleep each morning and meet him in the dream-space, and then I will be able to carry on with my day.

Oh my darling where did you go? How powerfully I feel you are somewhere, but not here. You come to me in another dream with a missing tooth and an unfamiliar red jacket; I know every single article of clothing you own, right down to the last sock and undershirt. Do you make friends and have companions where you are? I thought all you needed was us.

I dream I find you in Africa walking a red dust road. But it isn't you; this Ficre is fatter than the real one, a little layer of butter beneath his skin. I stand back and watch the figure hug the children to see if it is really him. It is him, yes; you came back; we found you. And soon we are fussing like the olden days.

But this Ficre, this Ficre—no, he is not my Ficre. In the dream, I ride a bus in Africa and note the quality of light, how bright it is, how wide the sky, and think of every time everyone ever said or wrote the phrase "under African skies." I thought I had to go to Africa to find him. But he was not there anymore. He left Africa.

The next morning, after the children are gone and I return to bed, I dream the house is full of unfamiliar people, and a wedding is soon to take place. The people are all white, and dressed in white. I don't know any of them; they float across my lawn like the cottonwood dander I once found beautiful. All the windows are wide open. I find the wedding caterer and say, this is my home! You don't belong here! But she cannot hear me. And then she says, to her co-worker, "This is the house where the famous chef from Caffé Adulis lived. He's upstairs now, and our chef wants the honor of meeting him!"

I take the stairs three at a time and there is Ficre. "The chef is coming to meet you!" I say, "Let me help you dress!" He hands me clothes and I help him into his pants and jacket.

He hands me a red jacket. I have never seen it before. He smiles at me, and a tooth is missing. I realize, then, what is true. This is how I know it is not him, not the living him.

He hugs me so tightly it takes my wind away. *I am so sorry, Lizzy, Lizzy, Lizzy my love.*

And then he is gone. My own keening wakes me. He will not come to my dreams again, not even to the edge. Soon, he is never in the garden when I go there to find him. He was truly there after he died, and now he is not.

Ten

The slim one who eats oatmeal and flaxseed is the one who dies, while the plump one who eats bacon unabashed stays alive.

The one who smokes does not get cancer or emphysema as his wife always feared he would but instead drops dead before he hits the ground, of cardiac arrest.

The one who has suffered, lives, and finds true joy in each day.

You watch the spot to see if it will grow, watch the spot in the sky and wish on the star but then it is an airplane. Things are not always as they seem. The slim, fit, vital man with clear brown skin and eyes and straight white teeth was in fact, as the doctors would later say, the proverbial ticking time bomb, with three of four arteries almost completely clogged, something no stress test told us. The brown mole he watched and fretted on his hip turns out to be nothing, a splotch of pigment.

Sometimes the smiling person is not happy, but Ficre

believed that your outside reflected your inside. He ate blueberries and stood on his head in yogic aspiration, faithfully walked the treadmill and pushed away cheese.

One cardiologist I spoke to after his passing says he believes unequivocally that the stress of growing up in war and being a refugee affected his heart.

Some who do evil live to a hundred. Ficre lived to exactly fifty, he who never did wrong and never told a single lie.

The earth that looks solid is, in fact, a sinkhole, or could be. Half of things are as they seem. The other half, who knows. This has always been true. But now I must know it.

Eleven

I first became a mother on a gray and misty spring day, April 18, 1998. This Mother's Day, my fourteenth, the midwife who helped bring both sons into the world writes me an email message to share her memories of what a devoted partner Ficre was throughout my two pregnancies and births. Solo and Simon, the loves of his life. They gave him body love until his last day to give him all the strength he would need for his journey.

I find a poem by Ficre for Solomon in my computer files and I understand as never before what the children saved him from:

> *The funk is loud, toxic. I am veiled*
> *In speed and shrill, clear, one note*
> *Screams. They are aware*
> *I race leaving all things behind*

Only to catch up with more things
To overtake. Speed.
I scream back, infected, up-lifted

"I see the moon daddy"
I hear
Every now and then
Yes we see the moon almost every day
Several times. "I see the airplane daddy"

We see as well
The lion, tiger, rhino, hippopotamus,
Donkey, bantam rooster, the hen, chick chick,
The alligator, the crocodile, the snake, the toad,
The frog, fish, bird, red bird, cat

Doggie, cow, sheep, goat, coyote, caterpillar,
Worms, butterflies, bees, ants, whales, sea lions,
Belugas, cars, trucks, homes and more homes

This is what it is like
To ride with my son
Seeing the invisible

My son
Who is 1 year and ten months

Who has all of his teeth
Who is peaceful
Who is full of wonders

And song.

Twelve

I feel certain I can wait forever for him to come back. I leave the light on in the living room, the light that faces the street. If I am patient he will come back. If I sit on the stoop through the night he will come at dawn. He would have waited forever for me; he never was not there waiting for me. I can wait and wait and wait, as long as it takes.

Gone on a trip? Hiding in the crawl space under the stairs? Visiting a sick relative? Around the corner, picking up milk and eggs? Sitting in a café lost in an esoteric book?

I will wait for as long as it takes for him to return to me. He will return to find the children grown tall, perhaps married, perhaps with children named for him. He will return to find me composed in my starched dress and head-bonnet, waiting in the same wood-framed domicile he'd left.

Last night I thought he came on a skateboard in my dream, but of course, it was not him. He turned and smiled to me and was someone else, and skated away.

I am getting older and he is not.

Thirteen

I have to go to the studio and make sure it is secure. There could be flammable materials, turpentine. I don't know what I will discover. Two of my beloved students from the art school say they will come with me, Ronny and Kenny.

When we first enter, the life force within the space literally brings me to my knees. He is utterly present, but of course he is not present. He has left the studio tidy and ordered. I begin to take in what is there—the hundreds and hundreds of canvases, not to mention the photographs, multi-media pieces, short animated films, charcoal and pastel sketches, and much more—I see that what he had been doing was creating an entire body of work, full and complete. I had seen each line and mark he ever made at some point, but taking in everything together is another thing all together. He left us with his eyes on the world.

Ronny and Kenny dispose of what needs disposing: dried, stiff, paint-soaked rags, semi-full tins of paint thinner. Then they photograph everything, inch by inch, which they later make into a collage for me. There is a painting on the easel he worked on his last day on earth. It is a horseman, in swift, energized brushstrokes, and he is racing off the canvas towards something unseen, lightning-quick.

Fourteen

A hurricane is coming and Ficre is not here. The children tend the property and become men, Solo on his stomach figuring out how to clean the detritus-clogged drains, Simon hoisting lawn furniture upside down and moving enormous holiday pumpkins against the house. Where are you, Fiki, I keep saying. Will this storm bring you back, blow you onto the doorstep, disheveled but here? Early on, Simon dreamed he found you. You had been locked in the box for two weeks and were hungry but fine. It was all a terrible mistake.

I am wondering about the forgetting. I remember my mother visiting when Solo was five months old, watching me change his diaper and dress him. Do you realize how much better you've gotten at that? she said, and I could barely remember the first days and weeks, the awkward folding, his baby body slithering in my hands. All I could feel was the moment we were in, in which I knew how to take care of my baby.

Ficre always changed the diapers fast and tidy.

We are doing better, I know.

I am not allowing myself full and deep sleep. I am vigilant. Sleep brings death too close.

You have not come to see me, Ficre.

Will the hurricane wind bring you back?

To be on the verge of tears for seven months straight, all day, every day.

Where are you? You are part of this storm, this wind, this rain, these leaves. Plants will one day grow from your bones in the Grove Street Cemetery, my empty dirt bed next to you.

I imagine your grave one day spontaneously covered with peonies, my favorite flower, the one you planted for me and which bloomed reliably on my birthday, May 30, every year.

Almost always you were strong and well and your step was light. But every few years, you'd contract a burning flu. I'd swaddle you in the fine white cotton blankets from Eritrea called *gabi* and hold you through the night as you sweated it out. I'd tend you.

Under Amy's hands, four days before you died, you surrendered when she rubbed your shoulders at the birthday party.

Under my hands, five days before you died, you were the same strong lover as always.

Ficre in the bright leaves that have been falling from the trees in the afternoon light.

Ficre everywhere, Ficre nowhere.

Ficre in New York City, sitting and watching the lights and writing haiku.

Fifteen

I dreamed we sat in chapel at the children's Episcopal elementary school. Every morning at St. Thomas's Day School began with the whole community gathering in that space. I felt the fullness of Ficre's body beneath his beloved cable-knit gray sweater ("I am an African highlander who loves a sweater," he would say); he was there next to me. We were singing the hymns with full voices: "Lift Ev'ry Voice and Sing"; "Sit Down, You're Rocking the Boat." Hundreds of origami cranes fluttered over the sanctuary. We made a joyful noise and believed in the power of communal song.

We left the church and walked hand-in-hand to the corner store. I could feel my hand in his, then as now. At the store, there was only a chicken wing and one pork chop in the meat case—out of milk, out of bread, out of eggs, the shelves eerily bare. The light changed. And then he was gone from the dream.

I cried so hard I woke myself. My bed, the bedroom, the house, was suffused with sorrow. Sorrow like vapor, sorrow like smoke, sorrow like quicksand, sorrow like an ocean, sorrow louder and fuller than the church songs, sorrow everywhere with nowhere to go.

Sixteen

What a perfect May morning this is, one where I imagine he would have risen before us, fixed his coffee, and gone out into his garden. He would have stood upon his mount and watered the rows, sorting his head for the day. How will we now plant the vegetable garden? How will we thin the rows? My children knew his love and so did I, always unwavering, always trained upon us. But oh, to have had a chance to say goodbye, to tell him again.

Why did I speak as I did at his fiftieth birthday? I said goodbye.

Why did he buy the lottery ticket with my name on it? Why was he so angry when he lost?

Why was the studio left so tidy?

I run into Father Peter in Whole Foods, which strikes me as a line in a joke: *A priest in a T-shirt and a Yankees cap is pushing a grocery cart in Whole Foods.* "I thought God brought you your food," I say, and we laughed. He married us, christened both children, and preached Ficre's soul to the other side in Saint Barbara church. He always made space for us as outsiders to the flock, as I was not raised Orthodox, and Ficre was a skeptic whose childhood church-going was a part of the cherished memories of his community upbringing, but not a religious practice he wished to continue in adulthood.

Who was the saint who attracted birds? I ask Father Peter.

He answers, *Saint Francis, who spread his arms like wings and a flock of birds landed there, doves, larks, sparrows, and owls. A crowd gathered and though they spoke many different languages, they all understood him. Saint Francis spoke Italian, but each of the listeners heard the Sermon of the Birds in their own language. Each bird repeated the words Saint Francis uttered, but each bird spoke in a different language so each listener could understand.*

Yes, I say, that's right, and I tell him a story from our family:

One day we all went to the chickadee forest in Cape Cod. I wasn't too excited; I'm a city girl and don't want birds coming close to me. As we wended deeper into the woods, Simon suddenly stood still on the path—he was only five—and stretched out his arms. Chickadees came and lit all over him, on his arms, on his shoulders, on his head. He stood very still and smiled, for what felt like a very long time, and the birds chittered in the quiet wood.

Then I told Father Peter how Simon had described heaven, having seen his father there.

Father Peter said, *You and Ficre were blessed to be artists who take in the world that way, and so your closeness was sanctified. And your children were blessed to have you as parents. And your sons will always be blessed to have had their father. That will never change.*

Then he said, *Don't ever let anyone guilt-trip you, or tamper with what you know of your sacred love.*

We hug, and I leave without buying anything, having received the sermon I clearly needed. So what if I didn't buy food, I thought. We'll eat cereal for dinner tonight! I feel fully in possession of Father Peter's words. The ones that shimmer I repeat to myself: *sacred love.*

Seventeen

May ends with my fiftieth birthday. I'd wanted to have a joint birthday party with Ficre, a hundredth-birthday party. In our New Haven neighborhood filled with old houses and intellectuals, people sometimes have hundredth-birthday parties for their houses, which feels very New England to me in a way that we are not. But the idea of our being one hundred together was magic.

I refuse to have my birthday. I'll sit this one out, I repeat. But Joanne insists, *you have to have a birthday*, and she and Amy make a small party for me where we feast in their home with our children, my parents, Mark, Tracy, and Alondra, dance hard to hip-hop the kids DJ, and then listen to a live chanteuse sing songs that make all the grown-ups cry. Joanne is right: you cannot stop your birthday from coming, so you might as well celebrate being alive.

I did not grow up in the black church, nor with the

Negro spirituals. Now I understand them as never before. Their poetry feels pure and profound. *I been in sorrow's kitchen and done licked out all the pots. Nobody knows the trouble I seen. Steal away to Jesus. I ain't got long to stay here.* I think of Frederick Douglass's great words that I have taught countless times:

"I did not, when a slave, fully understand the deep meaning of those rude and apparently incoherent songs.... The remark in the olden time was not unfrequently made, that slaves were the most contented and happy laborers in the world, and their dancing and singing were referred to in proof of this alleged fact; but it was a great mistake to suppose them happy because they sometimes made those joyful noises. The songs of the slaves represented their sorrows, rather than their joys. Like tears, they were a relief to aching hearts."

Slaves sing most when they are most unhappy, he famously wrote. Song raises and bubbles up as the only apt expression of this sorrow, the only possible bulwark against eclipsing grief.

I have not dreamed enough of Ficre because my subconscious is vigilant. I hope no one is fooled by my competence. The waters of sorrow continue to wash and wash.

The few safe zones are clear, as if infrared. Outside of those zones, there is free-fall.

The children are obsessed with stories in the sensationalist press of the coming zombie apocalypse, and flesh-eating creatures arisen from the dead. I brush it off but their beliefs persist.

My fiftieth birthday and flowers keep coming, cards, celebration, and love. One of us is still here.

You were supposed to be a hundred together, my mother says.

Eighteen

What does it mean to grieve in the absence of religious culture? I am, formally, Episcopalian on both sides—an Afro-Saxon—but was not raised going to church, though I spent much of my life until going to college studying ballet and modern dance at a studio in St. Mark's Church, performing with the company in services. Art is certainly my religion. I believe in the chosen family, especially as I get older. I believe in some kind of encompassing black culture that I am part of—"syncretic," to use the word Ficre liked—but I am also aware of the romance behind that sense of belonging. *I am feeling very Jewish*, I keep hearing in my head, thinking not of my actual Jewish Jamaican great-grandfather but rather about a wish for a religious culture that reveres the word and tells you what to do: Rosh Hashanah. Days of Awe. Invite the dead to Sukkot. There seems to be a poetic ritual for everything. I am not a black Baptist who will fall out in her grief and be lifted by the hands of her fellow parishioners. I am not an Eritrean

woman who goes through the house keening, *Ficre hawe,
Ficre hawe*, which means, Ficre, where are you? But I want
rules. I want the prayers to say every day for a year at dusk
and I want them to be beautiful and meaningful. I want
to sit shiva and have the neighbors come at the end of the
week and walk my family around the block, to usher us
into the sunlight.

Where is the village? I remember thinking when I had
my first child. Where is my sister? as I struggled to breast-
feed, for I have no blood sisters and my mother was of the
generation for whom baby formula was a miracle of nascent
women's lib. My mother-in-law showed me, kind of, though
we had no common language. We did have the common
language of motherhood and its many acts. Yet I was not
lonely without the village, without sisters who were also
mothers, because I had Ficre.

I hope you're not turning all Christian, Simon says, when
he comes home and finds me uncharacteristically blaring
gospel music. I am not, but I am listening to Mahalia Jackson in a whole new way. *How I got over, My soul looks back
in wonder*, I hear it for the very first time. The gratitude in
that song is what washes over me, the word *thank* repeated
over and over. My soul does indeed look back in wonder;
I had Ficre; I have Ficre; I have these extraordinary children; I have a village; I have an art-form; I am black; we
are African; we come from survivors and doers; my parents
are wise and strong; my body is strong; I was loved without

bound or condition; I exist in time and in context, not floating in space; my troubles are small compared to some; my troubles are not eternal; my days are not through.

"How I Got Over" was one of Dr. King's favorite songs, and Miss Jackson sang it just before the March on Washington, along with "I've Been 'Buked and I've Been Scorned." She spurred him on when he briefly stumbled as he gave that mighty speech—"Tell them about the dream, Martin!"—and her voice held millions of people aloft. Who we are as a people and how we make our way through sorrows that feel so profoundly intimate and personal but in fact exist on larger continuums, is what I hear in the song today. The first time she sings "How I Got Over" it is a question: How did I survive? But after that, the phrase is an answer, sung in varied inflection and redolent of varied meanings. This is how, this is how.

About halfway through the song Mahalia Jackson is stirred to clap and stomp, the song now fully in her body, carrying her over to shores unknown. And then, the song moves to astonishment: *How I got over!* In the absence of organized religion, faith abounds, in the form of song and art and food and strong arms.

When you become a family, you make common culture. Ficre and I shared cultures, folded into each other, and quickly made an indelible family culture. That we grew up around the world from each other seemed totally irrelevant. When he sleep-talked in Tigrinya, I remembered.

I remembered sometimes that our entire relationship, and most of his days, took place in his fourth language.

It is genuinely shocking to be jolted out of the world of our common culture into the world of our different worlds, and rituals around death and dying. He is no longer here as the ultimate medium or translator, the one who selected what mattered. There is only unalloyed culture, and no one to negotiate the treaties.

And the strange awareness that there was any culture other than our own.

IV

GHOST OF ALL BOOKSTORES

One

The day he died, the four of us were exactly the same height, just over five foot nine. We'd measured the boys in the pantry doorway the week before. It seemed a perfect symmetry, a whole family the same size but in different shapes. Now the children grow past me and past their father. They seem to grow by the day; they sprout like beanstalks towards the sky.

Week after week I continue to watch them at basketball practice with our beloved Coach Geraldine. I listen to how they deepen their voices to holler "BALL!" Coach G. tells Solo, "Get large!" or as his father told him, "Never be smaller than you are." Be large. I watch how the young men on the team intimidate each other on purpose, how they enact their masculinity, in each other's faces, controlled aggression that sometimes bursts over, how they manage the aggression. I watch them knock each other down and help each other up. I watch them master the codes of the court and the street. I watch them practice their swag. They are smelling themselves, as the expression goes, literally smelling their funk, feeling the possibility of their maleness. I watch their splendiferous gloating when they make a three-pointer, how they yell "BEAST!" to each other when they snatch a rebound. And I watch how they give each other skin for each job well done, this fellowship of beautiful young men, learning to be mighty together inside of this gym with an inspirational woman coach who loves them and is showing them how to be large, skilled, savvy, young men living fully in their physicality after their father's body so suddenly stopped working.

Simon's anklebones appear shiny at his pants' hems. He complains his feet hurt and indeed his toes have grown and are pushing against the ends of his shoes.

His growing seems avid, fevered. It feels like the insistent force of life itself. Ficre looked forward to seeing his sons grow beyond him. If I could hear him, I would hear him laughing his great laugh at this latest development.

Two

Simon tells me three dreams he's had in quick succession:

In the first, he goes down to the basement and finds Daddy sitting on the treadmill, rubbing his head and saying, Wow, I really bumped my head when I fell. In the second, he and his brother arrive at the hospital and I tell them, They did everything they could for him and then the last thing worked! And then Daddy comes out with a bandage on his head, smiling. In the third, Daddy is in heaven, dressed in the bright pink shirt he so loved. I'm having dinner with God tonight! he says. And I'm trying to grow a Fu Manchu mustache—you can do anything you want in heaven! In the dream, he told Simon he sits with Jackson Pollock in heaven and talks about painting, even though Jackson Pollock wasn't supposed to be very nice.

To love and live with a painter means marveling at the space between the things they see that you cannot see, that they then make. White canvas, blank walls, his vision.

Today I see him where he is not: outside my office window, dressed brightly, waving. I jump up and let him in the building. He has brought me green tea with honey and sits in my office reading something, anything, from my shelves while I finish my work before we go to the movies. I love being in your space, he says, like always. There he is where he liked to be, on my office sofa, reading any one of my books, pulled at random from the shelves. Tonight it is Teju Cole's *Open City*, wherein a recent immigrant from Nigeria walks the streets of New York, thinking, reading, talking, running into people, narrating what his new eyes see, ruminating brilliantly on questions of identity.

Rabbi Ponet writes about Jews as a book-loving people, and the erotics of the book. He imagines us dancing with the books we find sacred. I can see Ficre dancing with the books he loved. When he was a child one of his nicknames at Italian school was "mangia-libro," book-eater, he loved them that much.

I see him at home on the little red sofa, reading Primo Levi's *The Periodic Table*.

I see him on the rocking chair on the porch in Puerto Rico at Christmas, reading *The Black Count: Glory, Revolution, Betrayal, and the Real Count of Monte Cristo*.

I see him sitting across the aisle from me on the airplane, reading *Yoga Journal*.

When I open *The Black Women's Health Book*, which

he bought for me and was reading, a scattering of lottery tickets flutters out.

The Yale art historian Sylvia Boone is buried in Grove Street Cemetery. Her great work is called *Radiance from the Waters: Ideals of Feminine Beauty in Mende Art.* She was the first black woman faculty tenured at Yale, a history that feels close, as I am only the third. Her gravestone is a West African wonder in rosy marble etched with seashells and a Sowei mask she'd written about. Ficre and I would sometimes stroll there, sit, and talk. She was a kind of guardian angel of the African diaspora and its mighty ideas; her articulation of black beauty felt like a benediction. In her earlier book about traveling to West Africa—where Boone worked with Malcolm X, and Kwame Nkrumah, and W. E .B. Du Bois, and Maya Angelou—she wrote that travellers should always commit the "charming, hopeful, irrational" act of buying a lottery ticket in new countries. She called it "buy[ing] a chance." It will make you feel lucky, as if anything could happen, even when "you *know* you will not be there for the drawing."

Three

He had a scar on his hip from a dog bite in his childhood. Our first night together I kissed it and he breathed the most profound sigh and asked how did I know exactly where he wanted to be touched, that no one had ever touched him there. Our romance was like that, healing every old wound with magic disappearing powers until they were all tended. We lived out of time, nursed all injuries, shared all the stories and then were fortified and ready to go on with our life together.

At dinner, I ask the boys if they remembered that scar, and they do, and the scar on his hand from when he offered the dog a cookie. No wonder he was wary around dogs! We tell a funny story about how Daddy poked the stick in the donkey's ass and the donkey kicked his two hind legs in Daddy's stomach. African stories, stories with animals in them, stories in the backyard, stories with lessons, ghost stories, war stories.

We don't talk about the old scar on his head, which the

treadmill scraped clean off when he died. It is one of our shared nightmare images we wish we could un-see. The old scar was a three-inch, purple-ish ribbon across his scalp. "He fell off his bike," Solo remembers. "He told us, he fell off his bike and all of the streets of Asmara ran red with his blood." Simon has already dreamed his father's head clean and healed without the scar, and that, he says, is how you know Daddy is dead in the dream.

We three loved his head, and caressed it. We were the keepers and protectors of his dear brown head. We loved him with our hands on his head.

Four

I loved my friend
He went away from me
There's nothing more to say
The poem ends,
Soft as it began—
I loved my friend.

—LANGSTON HUGHES

I look across at his side of the bed as I wake with my mind racing with quandaries and I think, I miss my friend, plain and simple.

The boys and I go to Robert and Michele's for dinner. They are among the many dear people who have been feeding us. They've previously dropped off lentil soup, meat loaf, and Robert's gravlax, but now we feel we can make and keep a date, and spend an evening with people who will hold us tenderly.

Michele was another one of Ficre's Italian American

sisters. They would cook for each other and speak Italian in the kitchen, discuss the nuances of spinach with currants and pine nuts and the relative merits of pasta shapes: orecchiette versus creste di gallo, rigatoni vs. penne. Tonight, she makes spaghetti with a hundred onions, the most comforting and delicious dish I have ever eaten, which we slurp as though we've never been fed before, and talk about Ficre.

"I LOVE him," Robert says. "Not, I *loved* him. He IS my friend. I can still talk to him." Yes, I think, that is true exactly.

But the friendship part of marriage, that is the part that is enacted, that is the part for which you need the person present, and that is what I miss. Robert and Michele are long-marrieds and understand this absolutely. Yes, I still talk to him. Yes, if I still myself enough I can imagine what he would say to guide me. But that is not the same as friendship itself, and friendship in marriage is its own thing: friendship in a cup of tea, or a glass of wine, or a cappuccino every Sunday morning. Friendship in buying undershirts and underpants. Friendship in picking up a prescription or rescuing the towed car. Friendship in waiting for the phone call after the mammogram. Friendship in toast buttered just so. Friendship in shoveling the snow. I am the one you want to tell. You are the one I want to tell.

Ficre adored the long laughter and various "Girl"s that would punctuate my phone conversations with dear sister friends. He always wanted me to have those conversations by his side while he watched television or read. *I like to hear you laugh,* he'd say. Near him, is what I miss. And the near-voice of intimacy.

What did Lucille Clifton mean when she wrote that she was spoken to by a "voice from the undead past" in the poem "the light that came to lucille clifton"? What did the old folks mean when they said, "Every shut-eye ain't asleep, every goodbye ain't gone?" Isn't friendship all in the doing? If I cannot take a walk with you and talk my way to the other side of the dilemma, I am not enacting friendship. If I cannot tell you every little thing when I am preparing dinner and you have poured me a glass of wine, how are you my friend? "I loved my friend. He went away from me. There's nothing more to say."

Days later it feels like progress when I write to Michele for the spaghetti recipe. She replies:

Are we the only ones who crave this? I came home and made it tonight and we blissed out. OK, here's how to make the sauce for 1lb of pasta:

1. Cut 2 to 3 oz of pancetta into 1/4-inch dice—you should have 1 cup—and put them in a large sauté pan with 3T of olive oil. Turn on the heat and cook gently until the pancetta begins to brown.

2. While that's happening, slice four onions (red, white or yellow, or a mix) thinly (but not too thinly). When the pancetta has begun to brown, add the onions to the pan, salt and pepper them, and turn them several times in the oil. Put a lid on the pan, turn the heat as low as it'll go, and cook for 40 minutes or so.

3. While the onions are cooking, bring a big pot of water to a boil, add salt (2T). When your sauce is almost done, add your spaghetti to the water and cook al dente. (Really al dente. You want it to bite back. It'll cook more in the sauce.) Drain the pasta and add to the sauce with whatever water is clinging to it. Add more pasta-pot water to the pasta and sauce if need be.

4. At the last minute, add 3T finely chopped parsley and 1/3 cup grated Parmesan cheese to the pasta and toss. Serve in a heated bowl and pass more cheese at the table.

This is the best dish!! It'll make you want to throw rocks at other pasta dishes.

xoxoxoxo, M

As I make the pasta I remember Ficre in our kitchen teaching me how to more adeptly use a knife, to preheat a pan, to press garlic cloves so the paper jackets slip off, to simmer tomatoes until they turn sweet and roast beets until they are like candy. The boys and I eat our delicious spaghetti until sated. Our whole bodies are warm. Ficre is in our stomachs.

Five

We loved Jimmy Scott's version of the David Byrne song, "Heaven": "Heaven is a place where nothing ever happens." These days I picture heaven populated by the umber angels Ficre painted in abundance, but that seems too fanciful. I never truly believed in heaven and cannot manufacture it. Little Jimmy Scott's plaintiveness seems right when he sings "no-thing e-ver hap-pens." How better to describe the infinite solitude of the afterlife?

"When this kiss is over it will start again, it will not be any different it will be exactly the same," he sings. Each kiss is fixed. It is the same long kiss, but it will never change. That is the comfort, and that is the heartbreak.

One night at bedtime, Simon asks if I want to come with him to visit Ficre in heaven.

Yes, I say, and lie down on his bed.

"First you close your eyes," he says, "and ride the clear glass elevator. Up we go."

What do you see? I ask.

God is sitting at the gate, he answers.

What does God look like? I ask.

Like God, he says. Now, we go to where Daddy is.

He has two rooms, Simon says, one room with a single bed and his books and another where he paints. The painting room is vast. He can look out any window he wants and paint. That room has four views: our backyard, the dock he painted in Maine, Asmara, and New Mexico.

New Mexico? I ask.

Yes, Simon says, the volcano crater with the magic grass.

Ah yes, I say, the caldera, where we saw the gophers and the jackrabbits and the elk running across and Daddy called it the veldt.

Yes. Do you see it?

And I do. The light is perfect for painting. His bed in heaven is a single bed.

Okay, it's time to go now, Simon says. So down we go.

You can come with me anytime, he says.

Thank you, my darling.

I don't think you can find it by yourself yet, he says, but one day you will.

Six

Ficre stops coming to my dreams, so I lie in my bed after I have sent the children off to school and imagine my dreams instead. Half asleep, I picture him walking through the door with luggage as if from war.

Reunion at the front door: an acquaintance's bipolar son appearing on their doorstep after years in his vortex, shaggy, smelling, dirty.

To Sleep with Anger, the film I watched the night before he died, and the trickster from the South who knocks at the northern migrant's door.

The Eritrean saying that you can't walk by your friend's house without knocking on the door to say hello.

My parents, New York apartment–raised privacy-lovers, who hid from the knock at the door in their freestanding houses.

Would Ficre return trim in his army greens, a huge duffel bag slung over his shoulder?

Is he somewhere with amnesia from the blow to his head?

Would I scramble to make his favorite meal while the children pulled off his boots and washed his feet in a tin basin, as he washed the feet on the nuns who made pilgrimage past his home on the days leading up to Easter?

I can see it so vividly, Where have you been?

My life will be a trail of breadcrumbs wherever it takes me until I die.

But lo I have seen his body, so know this is a tricky mind. I have seen it.

Seven

I have not yet learned how to use our television DVR. One of the points of marriage is that you split labor. In the olden days that meant one hunted and one gathered; now it means one knows where the tea-towels are kept and the other knows how to program the DVR, for why should we both have to know?

I now learn the DVR and find traces of him in the programming. Under "Record Series," Melissa Harris-Perry's new show. Oh how he loved a smart black girl, and especially a cute one. Kundalini Yoga. *Nova. American Masters. Unsung,* just for me. I'd binge-watch his offerings (Lou Rawls! Donna Summer! Shalamar!). My Negro wife, he'd say, with the warmest of amused smiles.

Now I erase some of those settings to make room for new things: NBA All-Star Game, *Scandal, Chopped.* I erase *The Big C;* that show is over, and on it, the middle-aged wife died. The husband had a heart attack and lived. I watched the end of that show that Ficre and I started together without him, and wept, cursing the living husband who came back from the precipice.

He was never not thinking about us. Everything he touched contained his thoughts of us, including the alien television.

I speak on the phone for the last time I will need to to a cardiologist who explains to me what happened exactly as others have, based on his autopsy report: he was probably dead before he hit the ground, that he may have felt a bit sick beforehand but the event itself was like lightning, and would not have left time for fear or pain.

Then he tells me the story of the priest who had a heart attack on the pulpit while preaching the resurrection on Easter, and the church was next to the fire department, and they came instantly and helped him, and he lived, and then later told of going to the precipice. He saw his mother. It was peaceful and beautiful. He was sorry to come back.

I keep paying his cell phone bill for a year and a half afterwards, because I don't want to lose the text messages, but I don't have the heart to read and transfer them. The phone goes dead and gets lost somewhere in the house.

But then I find it, and it is time. Simon cries rainstorm tears when he sees the photograph on the phone of his father blowing out his birthday candles at the kitchen table.

Texts he sent at 2:08 p.m. the day he died, to one of our nieces, Luwam, about her mother's medical treatment.

A short bit later, texts with Solo, saying that he was waiting for the boys in the parking lot at school.

What a profound mystery it is to me, the vibrancy of presence, the realness of it, and then, gone. Ficre not at the kitchen table seems impossible. I draft my first meager poem in many months, a re-entry exercise:

FAMILY IN ¾ TIME

We are now a three-legged table,
a family of three, once a family of four.
We bring ourselves into new balance.
The table wobbles, but does not fall.

We are still a family of four, I think,
when we meet new people, and wonder
if Ficre is visible to them.
I keep the kitchen table set for four

and buy the same amount of food: four
salmon filets, eight thin chicken cutlets,
four miniature chocolate éclairs.
We are ready for when he returns.

I watch a short video the children took on Ficre's iPhone from the morning of his fiftieth birthday. He is asleep and I am circled around him, pretending to sleep, for I am in on the surprise. The boys bring a tray to our bed: a daffodil (from the garden; it is March 21), espresso pot, toast, white yogurt drizzled with golden honey, and strawberries. All of us in our bed eat together, everything important and true in that image. Solo is the cameraman. Simon tells joke after joke and the boys fall out laughing. One of them sings a song.

Eight

The language of flowers is not a language I grew up knowing. I grew up in the city, Washington, DC, the child of transplanted New York Harlem apartment people who did not know how to grow things. There were crocuses in springtime that my mother planted along the walkway of our townhouse, and I remember my grandmother—born in Selma, Alabama, and reared in Birmingham, then Washington, DC—advocating that we plant hardy pachysandra, which her sister in Durham used as groundcover.

As a little girl in Washington I liked to sit on the ground beneath the dogwood tree in our tiny front yard at 819 "C" Street Southeast and search for four-leaf clovers. Clover was all I knew of "flower"; that was the time I spent in "nature." A family joke was, they say I bawled when first placed on grass to crawl. At my elementary school, honeysuckle vines and mulberry trees grew surrounding the parking lot; my best friend and I would gorge at recess in springtime and imagine ourselves foragers in the wilderness.

Rain puddles seemed as significant as lakes or ponds. In our neighborhood in the Sixties when I was growing up, country people still lived on Capitol Hill. I'd see them in their front yards catching a breeze when our family would go for slow walks on weekend summer evenings. In their yards grew geraniums and others that I thought of as the province of black people, Negro flowers. Though as an adult I have rarely been without fresh-cut flowers in my home—even a fistful of dandelions in a water-glass—I did not begin to know flowers until I knew Ficre and we moved into our house.

Now, the first full spring after his death, the still lives he set in the garden emerge. A small composition rises in a corner by the driveway: a stalk of grape hyacinth, scientific name *muscari*, derived from "musk" referring to the intoxicating scent which Ficre knew was my favorite olfactory harbinger of spring. A rare, almost cocoa-colored tulip which I now learn were originally planted in the Arts and Crafts era to match those houses in the style of ours. A shiny, frilled, purple-black parrot tulip that feels as late Victorian as the time period of the house. The whole cluster forms a dark, strange, gorgeous little still life, as carefully made as Ficre's paintings, with histories and etymologies and referents that continue to unfold.

With each community of flowers in the garden, a story: white and pink-streaked peonies, which always, always blossomed on my birthday, May 30, his birthday gift to me each year. There was never not a peony clipped and in a short drinking glass to greet me on my birthday morning, its head heavy with morning dew and often a small beetle. This spring I learn our peonies are double blooming, the rarest and most revered by gardeners. Ficre did not see them achieve this status but he was more patient than anyone I ever knew by far, and knew they would come up in the future. This year, the peonies are magenta and white, and they blow open as big as toddlers' heads, and soon they are spent and rotten, their petals brown and withered in the ground. Over and done until next year.

I look along the corner of the house and see the purple and white climbing clematis—if stars could be violet these are violet stars—climbing across the side gate as they did up the fencing on Livingston Street. Once our friends Cindy and Dick came for dinner and Cindy walked through the garden and oohed and aahed at the clematis. How did he make it grow so abundantly? That was in the days when my sons called each other "Brother," as their names, and Bob Marley's gospel of diasporic love and righteousness played in their young ears each day.

And then, this morning, out the back: huge, ruffled, cream- and apricot-colored iris. I have never seen these before. I bring the boys to the window, one at a time. "Look," I say, "Daddy is saying hello to us," and he surely is. Through the stalks and the blooms come the touch of his hands on the bulbs. *Hi, honey*, I say, and I hear him say,

Hi, sweetie, and the hurt is completely fresh, the missing, the where have you gone. I do not feel comforted. And I am still bewildered, from the archaic, "wilder": to be lured into the woods, into some wildness of mind. Will I really never speak to him again?

I look again at the color of the iris. It appears in many of his abstract paintings. The New Haven Italian printers who manufactured a catalogue of reproductions of his book kept coming to the studio to make color corrections, because they said, "this color doesn't exist." It only existed in his paintings.

Ficre did not paint what he saw. He saw in his mind, and then he painted, and then he found the flowers that were what he painted. He painted what he wanted to continue to see. He painted how he wanted the world to look. He painted to fix something in place. And so I write to fix him in place, to pass time in his company, to make sure I remember, even though I know I will never forget. "This is a compound like the one I grew up in," he said, when we first visited the house. He squatted in the yard like it was land to be farmed. Compound: where families were safe, even when they were unsafe. Where families were families.

Flowers live, they are perfect and they affect us; they are God's glory, they make us know why we are alive and human, that we behold. They are beautiful, and then they die and rot and go back to the earth that gave birth to them.

Nine

Last night I went into a bookstore for the first time since Ficre died. Ah, I thought, I have been avoiding this, for he is the ghost of all bookstores. He is in the history section or the art section or the gardening section, reading books and piling them up. He would gather books for the children's library, more books than they could ever read, more books than I thought would interest them, and we would fuss about it. I'd suggest taking a few off the pile. He'd say, That makes the whole design fall apart. I'd say, where will we put them? He'd say, we'll get a bigger house, and then we'd laugh.

My darling you are not in this bookstore. Carrying home a bag of books I think of all the books I will never know about because you will not show them to me. I think of the loss of knowledge, all the things I will never know because you are not here to tell me. I cannot ask questions, I cannot be reminded. I can no longer say—though I still do—to the children, "That's a Daddy question," when they ask about the Peloponnesian War, or the Khmer Rouge, or Latin declension, or the quadratic formula, or how sink-holes are formed on limestone beds. You of all knowledge, you of all curiosity, god of books and deep knowledge, enemy of facile pronouncements, Ficre Ghebreyesus, ghost of all bookstores.

Ten

You were six and your brother was four, my mother said. The whole day passed, a lovely day, and at the end, I knew something was different, but I wasn't quite sure what. Ah, that's it! I said to myself. Nobody cried today! For the first time in six years, nobody cried!

We used to laugh at that story when my boys were young and the cries would come and go, dried up by the vanished sunlight like summer storms, fast-finished but ever-present.

I thought of that phrase tonight. "Nobody cried today." It is ten months, almost one year. I did not cry today. I cried yesterday. I may well cry tomorrow. But I did not cry today, and neither did either of my sons, though mostly I am the one who still cries. It is not an accomplishment, just an observation, but one that marks the passage of time.

The next day, Simon weeps, remembering the day his father died, remembering finding him, being the first to find him, wondering if dying hurt him, remembering that the last thing his father said to him before he went downstairs to the treadmill was a cheerful, "Check on me."

You did check, I tell him. And then I came, and then Brother. And we were there with him when his soul left the room. He was in his own home, and he was with us.

The tears subside, and melt into a few strong shudders.

A bit later, from the shower, Simon calls out to me, *I was a ten in sadness when I was crying, Mommy, but now I am a six.*

Whoops, he says, *it just went down to five.*

He comes out of the shower and puts on his pajamas.

Now it's just a three.

He brushes his teeth.

Now it's all gone, he says. *We were with Daddy when he died.*

Eleven

Today Ficre's younger brother Sahle reminds me that he can always hear his father's words, plainly—he was the same age as the boys when he left home and only saw his father a few times after. But the mold was formed. His father was in him, and is in him.

I look out at the backyard where Ficre sat and smoked and drank coffee and think to myself, he is not there. Not sitting in that chair. Is the goal to no longer see him there? Or to always see him there? Is the goal to replace these cherished vistas with new vistas?

I listen differently now to people who talk about the energy on earth that never dies. When we leave this house, what changes? When we return, do memories await us? Is it sad?

It is time to leave this house for a while and know that what is left of Ficre has a different form now. It is less sharp, more permeating, more essence, more distilled. It is less his body here, his body there, and more, he is the ground beneath us and the air we breathe.

I go to yoga for the first time since he died. Kundalini, chanting, rhythmic rocking, waving our arms in circles which they say opens our compassion. Compassion for others, compassion for yourself.

Compassion, waving my arms in circles.

Compassion, my capacious heart pumping.

Ficre's great heart, a heart so big it exploded.

He was not tired. He was not done.

Twelve

Though it seems impossible, the boys and I continue with a trip we have long planned, to see grown nieces and nephews with their spouses and young children in Geneva and Avignon. These nieces and nephews loved Ficre profoundly but we all know we must focus on our children, so our bruised souls make their way through the visit, walking through lavender fields and medieval French landscapes, going to an Alpine town to watch cheese being made, and preparing huge pots of spicy stews to eat at a long table underneath the trees. Then, Solo and Simon and I continue on to Joucques, a tiny village in southern France, to see Mona and Rashid and their children Dima and Sim and Lamya: part of my Chicago family to whom I brought Ficre, the miracle. Their family gathers here from Cairo and Marseille and New York and Barcelona and Chicago, and now there is a grandson, Dima's four-year-old son, Tariq.

The blazing sun there feels like life itself, especially when it still shines strong at six p.m. and we take our aperitifs on the patio. We walk down the dusty hill to the market. Mona makes a huge midday meal of grilled merguez and zucchini, rice, perfect tomatoes, wine. Oh how we sleep after lunch, the boys on their high Yemeni beds that Lamya, who is an archaeologist, has brought back from her work travels. Falling out sleep, the sleep of the ages. This feels like the first real sleep I have had since Ficre died, and after the first day I crave it. I sop it up and sleep and sleep and sleep.

And here, in Joucques, I read the first book I have read since Ficre died. There are books everywhere in this house of intellectuals. I pick up Tony Judt's *The Memory Chalet*. Ficre admired Judt's historical and political writing, but this is another sort of book, where he writes about his remembered childhood, dictated to an assistant after he woke from his dreams and Lou Gehrig's disease consumed all but mind and memory. To live in memory and in dreams is a cruel comfort. I read the book and then read more, as though discovering for the first time that I actually could read. Reading calls Ficre close.

"There is no one with whom I talked about a wider range of things than with Ficre," Rashid says. Sim is up on the roof here with his father, clearing branches seared by the summer heat. I see Rashid and Ficre on Edgehill Road surveying the property, as they loved to do, and deciding which branches overhanging the house needed to come down, and how to bring a pump into the flooded basement. Of course Ficre should be here, we all say. I talk with the young people I loved so much as teenagers, wonderful adults now, on the patio late at night while Solo and Simon sleep inside, and I feel home in my soul. They knew and loved me first, and then they knew and loved him, and we made a family.

Day after day I read books at a sitting and then fall asleep, and wake to *pastis* over ice and Tariq putting his head in my lap and entertaining us with theatrical French pronunciations of cheese names. There will always be children and there will always be old people. We spend most of our lives somewhere in between. When we produce the children, we get to be royalty for a short while—the world pulls out its chair for the pregnant woman—but soon we are once again worker bees, tending the little ones. "What is birth but death with complexity" wrote the poet Michael Harper. The beginning, the end, and most of the time in the middle.

Thirteen

I begin to feel I am carrying around a Santa's sack of gifts because of all the things I know that Ficre thought and felt. I know these things, just me, only me. He gave them to me every single day, all day. I was his person; he told me everything he thought. I run into one of the town yoga instructors in a coffee shop, reach into my invisible bag, and tell her how much Ficre respected her teaching, the care of her adjustments, how he came home one day from her class thrilled that he had done a headstand for the first time. I run into a neighbor and tell her Ficre thought she was beautiful and foxy, and had planned to make butterscotch pot de crème sprinkled with fleur de sel to delight her when she and her husband next came for dinner. I tell her about how amazed he was by the sous-vide egg she made when we ate at their house: an egg with an unctuous yolk and a crisp panko and smoked paprika exterior, like nothing he had ever seen or imagined.

I tell a colleague from the music department how much

he enjoyed talking to her about her expertise on the gamelan as they waited for the kids at the music school. Gamelan, didgeridoo, korari, the world's musical instruments fascinated him, and he always wanted to learn one or the other. I tell a friend, Ficre loved the conversation you had at the natural food market with him about the basketball player Jeremy Lin's winning streak with the New York Knicks, "Lin-sanity," which captivated our house for the few weeks it lasted. Ficre believed utterly in your gifts, I offer, to a niece who is finally pursuing the arts as we always thought she should. Ficre told me you were the mother he would most trust with our kids, the only house where he would let them sleep. Ficre didn't usually like potato salad but he would happily eat your potato salad every day. Ficre loved you like a sister. To poet friends: Ficre kept your book in the studio and we had a tug-of-war when your most recent collection came out—he swiped it from my bedside table. There is one friend I have not yet told, He was reading your book the day he died. It was the last book he read.

Fourteen

A year later, it is time to make decisions in the studio. It has been photographed exactly as he left it, each table surface a still life of his artist's practice, each palette a painting unto itself. Key Jo has sorted paintings according to size, dusted and labeled all 882 of them, plus the sketches, and the photographs, and the small metal sculptures.

We will put aside unused supplies to sell to art students and give to artist friends: rolls of pulpy paper, unopened tubes of fine oil and acrylic paint, tables and chairs and two-by-fours and PVC pipe and wire and glue guns. Coconut shells and the woven rush mats called *mishrafat* for cooling roasted coffee. And then I will figure out what to save in a few labeled boxes that will read "Daddy's studio," for the kids to do something with or not one day.

Anticipating throwing away his paintbrushes makes me queasy. They are somehow biological, his DNA in the brush fibers. I find a box of the very best paintbrushes, which are made of sable. I learn they have a natural taper, which forms a point that painters prize. Some brushes are made of squirrel, some hog bristles, some of faux camel hair—for camel is too woolly and curly to make a good brush—ox, pony, and goat. Ficre and I never talked about this, but as I learn about paintbrushes I chuckle, for I know he knew everything I am now learning and know he found it fascinating. It feels like there is so little he did not share that he knew, but of course each of us is infinite. The qualitative hierarchies of paintbrushes is something I learn from him after he has died. He is not here to teach me, but I would not have learned it without him.

The sable is a species of marten. Every contemplation of Ficre is a foray into learning something I did not know before. My friend Elena, who I have not seen since Ficre's passing, comes through town. She reminds me of the first night Ficre and the boys and I went to dinner at her house and how Ficre got blissfully lost in the maps in their antique atlas. He was man of maps and atlases; he was a cartographer and a cataloguer; he was a squirrel with nuts in his cheeks.

He would have known about the various animals that are used to make paintbrushes, and have had preferences. He was a connoisseur, I am an epicure. Connoit: to know. Epicureans take pleasure like no others, but are materialists. I am sometimes a sybarite. And surely, attachment is suffering.

The paintbrushes, I feel, contain his DNA, and so there feels something wrong about throwing them away. But I cannot keep them; they are stiff with paint, certainly unusable, unlovely though interesting.

I have long been obsessed with the story of the frozen woolly mammoth, how scientists used a blow-dryer to thaw him and extract DNA from his fur. Now I read they have found liquid blood inside a 10,000-year-old woolly mammoth. They will extract the DNA and eventually fertilize and plant an egg inside an elephant.

I want to know every single thing about woolly mammoths. I have to find a paleontologist. Knowing more and more, though, can block the passageways to feeling.

Ficre's DNA is everywhere in the studio, and in the paintbrushes he held for so many hours.

We can neither save nor harvest it. There is no frozen sperm. The being we would clone would never be Ficre.

I tell Elena; I saw the body without him in it; I know there are souls and bodies are just bodies; I saw his body after the soul had left and understood that our bodies are vessels the souls visit.

And then they go where?

Or are they finished? Are our bodies unique hosts?

Every day I hear music he would have loved. Today it is Esperanza Spalding's "Apple Blossom," and as I listen closely I realize it is about a man whose lover has died. The refrain:

> *Now he stands beneath the apple blossoms*
> *Every year where they used to go walking.*
> *And he tells her about the summer and the autumn,*
> *The winter in his heart,*
> *And their apple blossoms.*

We used to walk together in Grove Street Cemetery—where he is now buried where I will one day join him—and sometimes sit beneath trees and speak quietly and carefully about important things just between us. "Winter in his heart" seems the truest and most literal description of how my chest feels from weeping for him.

After the studio, I clean deeper in the never-ending house, facing it bit by bit. I clean my pantry cabinets and find expired baking supplies: Ficre was excited about the bread-maker that Amy and Joanne gave us, so in his fashion became a bread-making amateur expert. He bought two brands of yeast and powdered milk solids. He read how to make sourdough starter. He bought wheat and white and rye and spelt bread flours, rice flour to experiment with gluten-free bread for Amy and Joanne's daughter, Marina. I throw all the expired flours away. They smell ever so slightly rancid, but not unpleasantly so. They smell biological. I am reminded that grain is alive, a host for bacteria. Things grow and live in it.

And then, more things go, the makings of confections he will never prepare.

Away, almond paste, for the marzipan-apricot tarts he promised.

Away, date and beet sugars.

Away, unsweetened coconut, which seems to have turned to grit, with which he made his ethereal shrimp barka, the stuff of legend.

As I purge, upstairs my student Kathryn downloads literally thousands of CDs from his studio and loads them onto something in outer space called a cloud. All the music he listened to, his sonic DNA. Kathryn was in the lecture class "African American Art Today," to which I returned a week after Ficre died to deliver a final lecture. Somehow I wrote it; I needed to write it, and go to them, my beloved community of students for thirteen intense weeks, and deliver their last class of the semester. After the lecture, each one of them lined up and solemnly shook my hand, or hugged me. Not one broke down and neither did I; they conferred their strength to me; they held me aloft.

Here is how I ended that lecture:

"Don't forget to feed the loas" serves as an entreaty
or opening salvo and refrain in Ishmael Reed's
great novel *Mumbo Jumbo.* The phrase articulates
the imperative to remember to honor the deity-
like ancestral forces that guide us through our

contemporary lives. The offerings on their altars may be fruit or flowers, chicken or wine; when taken metaphorically, offerings may also be found in the form of art and the calling of names that honors our dead and keeps them near.

This is Jason Moran's "Cradle Song." Listen carefully: (I played it). "Cradle Song" appears on the album "Artist in Residence," which was recorded shortly after the pianist's dear and influential mother died of cancer, a relatively young woman. "Cradle Song" is an elemental solo that sounds something like a mature student's variation on a simple piano exercise, perhaps a variation on a Chopin etude before the student has learned it well enough to play it fully fluently. It includes the recorded sound of intense pencil writing. According to Moran, this is meant to represent his mother's writing and note-taking during his music lessons when he was a child. This very very small quotidian sound—the presence of his mother's hand—is called back into the music, called across the line between life and death and in that sound, she is present. The sound of the writing is the second instrument on the recording; the piano solo is, then a duet, with the mother who was by her son's side as he learned to become a piano player. If the presence of the mother taking notes by her young son's side is what moved him forward and accompanied him as an apprentice, its sound on the recording is what enables him to make music after she has died.

Art replaces the light that is lost when the day fades, the moment passes, the evanescent extraordinary makes its quicksilver. Art tries to capture that which we know leaves us, as we move in and out of each other's lives, as we all must eventually leave this earth. Great artists know that shadow, work always against the dying light, but always knowing that the day brings new light and that the ocean which washes away all traces on the sand leaves us a new canvas with each wave.

It's a fact: black people in this country die more easily, at all ages, across genders. Look at how young black men die, and how middle-aged black men drop dead, and how black women are ravaged by HIV/ AIDS. The numbers graft to poverty but they also graph to stresses known and invisible. How did we come here, after all? Not with upturned chins and bright eyes but rather in chains, across a chasm. But what did we do? We built a nation, and we built its art.

And so the black artist in some way, spoken or not, contends with death, races against it, writes amongst its ghosts who we call ancestors. We listen for the silences and make that art. "Don't forget to feed the loas," Ishmael Reed wrote, and so by making art we feed the ancestors, leave water and a little food at the altars we have made for them, and let them guide the work. We listen; we hasten to create.

Survivors stand startled in the glaring light of loss, but bear witness.

The black folk poets who are our ancestors spoke true when they said every shut eye ain't asleep, every goodbye ain't gone.

That is the context in which I met Kathryn. For these last months she has dozens of times asked, *how can I be helpful*, at home, in the studio, in my office at school.

So now, day after day she comes here with two huge iced coffees from Dunkin' Donuts, one for her and one for me, and goes up to her station, puts in her earbuds, and cheerfully downloads the music for hours in a row, working her way through each box, learning this man she never met but who she now knows through his paintings, his space, his music, and his family: everything he left on earth.

V

THE PLUM BLOSSOM

One

Our house is unusual amongst its neighbors: people don't reside here long, in a community where professors buy these lovely homes and tend to stay forever. When Ficre and I chose the house at 150 Edgehill Road we felt we could see our entire lives in front of us, our grandchildren coming there, sleeping in their father's childhood rooms left intact. We searched for a table big enough to accommodate feasts of friends and extended family in the dining room I had painted a color I called "Venetian pink," for Ficre. We relished our role as Command Central.

We would live here but two years as a family of four, and then a year and four months and fifteen days as a family of three.

When a previous family lived here, Archbishop Desmond Tutu spent a night as a guest. With other occupants, we're told, Thornton Wilder conducted playwriting workshops in the great room that faced the backyard. Our family celebrated two New Year's Days with black-eyed peas and song. Ours was a house where the piano was played, a house where we sometimes read poetry at the dinner table and once served a coconut cake so delicious it made our guest weep at his grandmother's memory. A house where the traditional Eritrean *guayla* was danced in a circle, and where friends danced to funk 'til the windows steamed up.

It was a house where Ficre made red lentils, and spicy beef stew, and Bolognese, and the curried vegetable stew alitcha, and I made eggplant parmigiana and chicken cotoletta Milanese in the manner he taught me, and pesto from basil in the garden, and blueberry küchen and chocolate Pavlova and chocolate chip cookies with sea salt sprinkled on top. *Casa dolce casa*, the boys and I now say when we walk through the door, as he did each time we returned from our travels.

Ficre was expressive and eloquent in Italian, his third language, and New Haven had a ready supply of Italian interlocutors. Connecticut has the second highest Italian population of any state in the U.S., after Rhode Island. In New Haven, Ficre spoke some Italian most days. Carlo the carpenter would come and visit when we had just moved into our apartment on Livingston Street. I loved being a pretty, pregnant housewife, making him perfect espresso and serving it in the red enameled cups with tiny almond cookies. Carlo was an elder, full of aches and pains and complaints and off-color stories he'd tell Ficre when I left the room. He made Ficre laugh hard. We'd asked him to make a dining room table for us, of Ficre's design. For months he'd come and talk over cups of espresso with Ficre about the table, which was always going to be ready, *presto, presto.* We continued to eat cross-legged on the floor, serving our guests on an elegant Scandinavian mid-century modern coffee table that Ficre had found at Goodwill for ten dollars and proudly refurbished until the clean lines were revealed and the inlaid wood gleamed. One day just before Solomon was born, Carlo called Ficre with great excitement: I have it for you! *È pronto!* And he came over not with the dining room table but with a handmade rocking cradle for the baby, with his signature carved into the wood on the underside.

I have a dream where time is all a jumble. First, I am in Ficre's studio, and he has already died. I discover three paintings he has made of an Italian American folk creature, a jumping baby of sorts. In the dream, it is summer early light and the studio is already getting hot.

Then Ficre is alive, and up and out of the bed for his coffee at four thirty, when the birds began to sing. He comes bouncing in the door from the studio at the end of his day, excited to be working on the Italian paintings. Hello, sweetheart. A kiss on the lips. You are back, my darling, as if nothing ever happened. He sets to making red lentils for dinner.

We live right across the street from his studio in this dream. Everything we want is at hand: work, kitchen, gazebo, each other, summer light. How can I leave the peace of this house? I wonder. I have never lived in a house so beautiful. I have never felt so content.

When I wake I know, all of a sudden, that it is time for us to leave. Ficre isn't here anymore. Ficre is not here. I can make his red lentils anywhere.

SPICY RED LENTIL & TOMATO CURRY

Author: Ficre

Prep time: 15 minutes

Cook time: 4 hours 20 minutes

Total time: 4 hours 35 minutes

SERVES: 4–6

Don't be scared off by the long cook time—for the most part, once you've taken care of the chopping, all you'll need to do is check on this dish occasionally as it simmers. To cut down on cook time, you can also use store-bought vegetable stock rather than making your own (you will need 2–3 cups). A note on tomato passata: although it isn't incredibly common in the United States I've found it at Whole Foods and another grocery store in the area. It's a tomato purée similar to tomato paste and tomato sauce—the main differences are that the tomatoes in the purée are uncooked, with no additional ingredients added, and it's not cooked down like tomato paste. If you can't find it, you can certainly substitute tomato sauce or crushed tomatoes for a slightly different flavor.

INGREDIENTS

For the Stock:

2 heads fennel

2 heads kale

1 yellow onion, cut into large pieces

2 large carrots, cut into large pieces

1 stalk celery, cut into large pieces

4 cloves garlic, finely chopped

For the Tomato Curry Sauce:

24 oz can tomato passata

2 carrots, chopped

3 cloves garlic, finely chopped

2 tablespoons curry powder

½ teaspoon cayenne

½ teaspoon paprika

2 cups dry red lentils

¼ cup fresh cilantro, chopped

Salt to taste

INSTRUCTIONS

1. In a large heavy pot, combine the first 6 ingredients and enough water to cover the vegetables by about a half inch. Allow stock to simmer for 4 hours.

2. After the stock has been simmering for about an hour, you'll want to start making the tomato curry sauce. Combine the tomato passata, 2 chopped

carrots, 3 cloves chopped garlic, and the spices in another large heavy pot and allow to simmer 3 hours.

3. Add lentils to tomato curry sauce and let simmer 20–30 minutes more, adding stock as needed to thin it out (about 2–3 cups). The mixture should be thick and creamy, not soupy or dry.

4. Stir in fresh cilantro and remove from heat. Season with salt to taste. Serve lentils alongside basmati rice.

Two

I come out of my first Pilates class exhilarated, blood flowing, stretched and tall. It is the first time in ages I lose myself and forget; my tears come fast and sting just after I think, *I cannot wait to get to the phone to call Ficre and tell him.*

Rilke surprises me, how true and contemporary he feels in *The Book of Hours*, poems which he wrote as received spiritual messages or prayers:

> *Let everything happen to you: beauty and terror.*
> *Just keep going. No feeling is final.*
> *Don't let yourself lose me.*
>
> *Nearby is the country they call life.*
> *You will know it by its seriousness.*
>
> *Give me your hand.*

For Rilke, God is the companion, the hand the reader is exhorted to take. Ficre is not my God; neither do I know who God is. But I find this force in art, poems, and the community I have made.

When we met those many years ago, I let everything happen to me, and it was beauty. Along the road, more beauty, and fear and struggle, and work, and learning, and joy. I could not have kept Ficre's death from happening, and from happening to us. It happened; it is part of who we are; it is our beauty and our terror. We must be gleaners from what life has set before us.

If no feeling is final, there is more for me to feel.

Three

How much space for remembering is there in a day? How much should there be? I think about this in my poetry. I don't want to be a nostalgist. Yet I feed on memory, need it to make poems, the art that is made of the stuff I have: my life and the world around me.

I am grateful for the tug of the day that gets us out of bed and propels us into our lives and responsibilities; memory can be a weight on that. And yet, in it floods, brought willfully, or brought on by a glimpse, a glance, a scent, a sound. One note: the timbre of his voice.

There will never be goodbye. And yet it will close something down, because we have moved to New York, and I feel its urgent press further away from me, even as I know the grieving continues, a huge, intricate, multi-branched coral, sharp and beautiful at the same time.

Did we leave him in the garden? Did we leave him in the Grove Street Cemetery?

The day we have packed the car, turned the key, and are

leaving town, we've planned to visit the cemetery but are delayed at a doctor's appointment. The cemetery closes. Mr. Cameron, who has been the caretaker forever and is probably ninety years old, comes at six a.m. seven days a week and closes the gates at three forty-five.

"It's okay," Simon says, to Solo's and my upset. "If we can't leave now, we can never leave."

And then he says, "The grave reminds me of Daddy's death, but I want to remember Daddy's life."

I tell them no one, not even I, can tell them when or how often they should visit their father's grave.

For the gravestone, we'd picked red India marble, from which we also had a bench made. I was aware, as we picked the bench, that the site was a double plot where one day my children would bury me next to their father. We picked one of his painting's wide-eyed, neo-Coptic angels and the engraving artist etched it onto the stone. On the other side are etched Ficre's words, from a small painting he made for our bedside: "I wake up grateful, for life is a gift."

"Oh beauty, you are the light of the world!" was the quotation we chose for the bench by the side of the grave, from a poem by Derek Walcott my teacher, whose words Ficre and I revered. The exaltation with which we met, and beauty itself, the thing we both chased and tried to re-create in our work, that which lights the world and its darkness that he understood so well. The poem says it better than any scripture.

Beauty is the beloved, and beauty is beauty itself, in its natural form and as made.

Ficre's paintings work from natural beauty—so many boats on the water, so many horizons—but also from a profound imaginative space. There, the shadow of a fish, but an impossible fish, going against the tide, in its own inexplicable direction. Ficre went his own way, made his own course.

As I sit alone with these words, I think about how brave he was in so many ways, and how brave he was to go into that studio every day with his demons and his angels, and labor to put them on canvas. *Nulla dia sine linea*, No day without a line, is the motto at the Art Students League, from Pliny the Elder, derived from the Greek painter Apelles. The devotions.

While packing I find photographs that he took. His camera lingers on an eight-year-old boy's hand, zooms in closer so we can see the words in the book the nine-year-old is reading, which is *The Borrowers*. The landscape out the window on a family sojourn zooms by, blurs, like this all does, but with flashes of sharp clarity. He looks closer at the hand so now he shows us the pores. He loves his wife's red pocketbook and red suede gloves. He takes pictures of the graves of the great Russian artists buried in Venice: Igor Stravinsky, Serge Diaghliev, Joseph Brodsky. He keeps looking, keeps taking pictures, and with each, his intimacy deepens. There is another picture of one of the boys' math books, a close-up of a page. It starts with a word problem: "Anna purchased three yards of fabric." And then the numbers, and the markings made fascinating by his camera.

He probably played those numbers. Yes, he loved the lottery. The last days of his life he was agitated about the lottery, kept saying he had to win it for me, leapt up to go buy more tickets and sat working their magic.

And what did Ficre see in me? Why did he come sit next to me and talk to me in the café that day? I'd just cut off all my hair, hair that went well past my shoulders; I started fresh; I was newly mown; my head belonged only to him. Time stretched and stretched; I went to him and then stayed.

I learned about Eritrea, the little country that could, and then we mobilized in the border wars of '98, did as much as we could, took in relatives.

Reading about a mother chef whose daughter becomes a chef, I think about taste and how it is developed, but is also as particular as sexual desire. How does what we like develop? The particular biology of the point at which my back breaks into sweat, or how I like to be touched, is as idiosyncratic as how much salt you like. Ficre did not salt, proudly. Simon loves salt, eats it, like my mother, who eats a whole bag of potato chips on the way home from the store. Ficre's hand on his mother's elbow at the stove, tipping the clarified butter ladle so more goes in the pot. More, more. How his body was made, how it broke down or did not break down fats. He developed cholesterol on blueberries and yogurt, even as his wife did not while eating high on the hog.

High cotton. We lived in emotional high cotton for a while.

Now I look back from forward. Something is fading, not the memory of him but the press of memory, the urgency of writing, the closeness of him. He is somewhere in the atmosphere, but also not. He is fifty and I am fifty-one. He is smiling in the green backyard; now his garden does not grow tall, does not grow at all. He is a photograph in the living room; he is, for the moment, still.

But he was always still in a certain way, a north star, a compass, who was loyal and predictable. I must have needed that; I used to joke with my mother that if my father said he would pick you up at ten and it was ten-oh-one, you'd know he was dead, he was that punctual, therefore that reliable. My parents never don't call back, don't reply, fall off the map, check out, and neither did Ficre, ever. Even in our worst moments, he was central, there, rooted at home and in us.

I never once doubted him, because that is how he made me feel. So I walk forward knowing I was loved, and therefore am loved.

Four

May 2011. Jason Moran and Me'Shell Ndegocello played Fats Waller, and we danced all night at the Harlem Gatehouse.

Was it true that dancers moved among us holding outsized papier-mâché masks on sticks?

Was it true that Me'Shell said to you from the stage, Look at you, brother-in-pink, loving on your woman like that?

Was it true Bobby O. was there in a cream-colored jacket and a papi lindo hat?

That night we danced in a fever, in a dream. The professional dancers came and took me by the hand and led me to the hypnotizing floor. It was the start of spring, blowsy and humid, incipient.

New York New York, big city of dreams.

Two springs later I am searching the earth for you, four corners, finding you in a seashell in my underwear drawer, oregano and chives coming up in the winter garden after a few warm days, the pink argyle sweater folded in a cedar trunk. No—that is the sweater we buried you in.

The winter garden is razed now, cleared, and you are no longer there, not there this spring.

April 1, April 2, April 3, April 4.

No, start counting at your birthday party, March 30, March 31—

No, start counting on your birthday, when we brought you coffee and etan in bed.

March 21, your fiftieth birthday.

Beloved.

Five

Leslie and Douglas give us a welcome-to-New-York party at their home in Brooklyn. We eat hummus with pomegranate seeds scattered over it, kibbeh, and Italian butter cookies. The Palestinian food comes from Bay Ridge and the cookies, from a venerable Italian bakery a few Brooklyn neighborhoods over. We drink fizzy scarlet Lambrusco, fall and summer together in each delicious slurp.

Friends appear from hither, thither, and yon. New ones, old ones, former classmates, former students. Beloved former students all grown-up are one of my favorite categories of people in my life, the greatest reward of a long teaching career. Ficre loved that I was a teacher, and always welcomed my students to our home.

Vincenzo and Alex come, with their two baby daughters. Vincenzo and Ficre loved each other. Vincenzo is the Sicilian husband of my friend Alex. Since Ficre died, the silly phrase "bromance" has come into fashion, and had it been current when he and Vincenzo met, Alex and I might have used it to describe the instantaneous pull our husbands felt to each other. Both artists, both soulful, both woman-worshipping monogamists, both aesthetes, both fixers and makers, both uncensored, both un-pretentious, both similarly self-effacing and similarly dramatic, both creatures of the nest, both passionate cooks and eaters.

We are seeing Vincenzo for the first time since Ficre's death, as he was out of the country when that happened and he and Alex have had two girls back to back in the interval. Alex came to the funeral hugely pregnant and I remember the urge to protect her as I saw the sorrow on her face.

Bella! Vincenzo says, taking my face with both hands and kissing me in greeting, and I hug him and break contact quickly because I know if I linger for even a moment we will cry.

Eh, the boys are beautiful, amazing! he exclaims. *I told them to move around, to stop sitting in their chairs like the aunties.* He is large and funny, voluble and direct. The last time they came to visit us, he and Ficre lay on the ground under a flowering dogwood tree that Ficre had planted and drank their wine and laughed and talked in Italian, sometimes holding hands. *Fratello* this, *fratello* that. Bromance.

As they leave the party, Vincenzo is draped with his girl-babies, with their loose curls and pierced ears and confectionary dresses. Like Ficre, he is a Pied Piper with children. He grabs each boy by the scruff of the neck and kisses them hard on each cheek to say goodbye. I think, no one outside of the family has kissed my sons quite like that since their father died.

We loved Vincenzo the best, the boys say to me later as we do the excited post-mortem of the welcome party. He made us think of Daddy.

Six

Ficre, you would love this macchiato: perfectly smooth, strong but not sharp, fortissimo but shy of bitter, with a sexy plouf of milk foam dead center in the tiny white cup. You would love this marble-top Italian cafe on the Upper West Side, as you loved the Upper West Side and all its nations and pleasures and haimishness. Do you remember, I want to say, when you took me to the burger place on Broadway you loved so much? You shared everything you had with me, the infinity of your interior space, every little discernment and opinion. Such is love. Thank you my darling, thank you.

On the every-varied streets of New York, I see people who remind me of him in glances: Ficre elderly, in a favorite overcoat and a gentleman's hat. Ficre an African man walking the city. I see a lovely bald brown head, or a slightly springing stride. He moved lightly and valued light-footedness, as he valued *sotto voce*. How he despised needlessly loud voices. Flashes of him in this complex metropolis, but he is not here.

Our niece Melay sends me a Google sound recording of a voice mail message from him sent in the months leading up to Easter. *Hi sweetie, I called about our Lenten lunch date. How about we make a dish together of red lentils? It takes five seconds to make such a dish. Lizzy will be home at five.*

I wonder if these memories are finite, which is why I keep writing them down. The basket of remembrance has three sides; one is open; can it tilt and spill out? Nothing more goes in the basket, my life with Ficre is over.

Except it is not. Except how I keep coming to know him again and again in the paintings, and in this writing, and in my mind. Traces are everywhere and unexpected. I come across an interview with Ficre that a young woman did for her food blog, "Dramatic Pancake." He teaches her how to make red lentils. He was a reluctant interviewee, but when he answered her three questions, he spoke from his center, and described to her himself in our world:

Three Quick Questions...and Ficre's Answers

It's your last meal. What do you have?
Probably this dish. It's a very good dish. There are many other things that I could have made that remind me of my parents, but I think this one is the best.

Your kitchen is burning down. What's the one thing you grab?
This work of art right here (motioning to a watercolor painting of a pig sitting beside a giant flower vase, on the top of a hill). Our son Simon made it when he was eight or nine years old—we call him our little surrealist. Everything else in here is replaceable, but Simon is never going to be eight or nine again and paint this same painting.

Do you have a favorite cookbook?
I'm not sure—is it okay not to have an answer? My wife uses most of the cookbooks. She loves Nigella Lawson, says she's a diva. I must admit that *How to Be a Domestic Goddess* is a very, very smart book. However, in general, I'm not a big believer in recipes. I find them a little controlling of one's energy.

I catch a glimpse of myself in a shop window as I run to catch a light on Broadway. There is my bottom, indisputable and proud, and there are my sturdy legs hard at work. "*Douba, doubina,*" I hear Ficre say. *Douba* in Tigrinya means "pumpkin," and as he used it was a term of affection for a curvy person, what black folks call "thick," or "brick house," but sweeter. Eritreans are very direct in describing a person's physical characteristics. If someone has some extra weight, they might be called "plumpy," to their faces. It is merely descriptive.

When first we met, we told each other about every single lover, every crush, every assignation, every heartbreak. When I told him about the one I loved most before him, who came after disastrous heartbreak, he says, "Bless him for loving you when you needed it, for healing you, and for preparing you for me." Everything was told! Then we could begin something new.

Seven

Every morning and every night I open and close my eyes to Ficre's painting *Visitation*. It allegorizes our first meeting in the State Street studio, when I walked through the "Foster Kindness" door into my future. In the painting, a man and a woman meet with offerings. From the woman, scarlet red tomatoes, her own fecundity held in cupped hands at her womb. She is wearing all white: the white of the Yoruba goddess Yemaya (with her blue nearby in the background), and the white of Obatala, the creator of all human bodies. The solemn brown man humbly offers an eye on a plate. That is what Ficre gave to all of us, his eyes on the world. We stand inside of him and have the privilege of seeing out as he did. The eye is also an icon, a protective evil eye that a caretaker offers his coming family. As in so many of his paintings, he has created a spirit house.

Though the pair is meeting for the first time, they are surrounded by the images of the children they will soon have, and their sons are painted as angels, for in Ficre's work, there are angels everywhere in landscapes where ancestors are conjured and present.

A curtain of flowers rains down over the woman's space, illuminating her. *Visitation* has Ficre's characteristic sense of what Amy called in his work "tutto" naming a kinship with the Italian artist Alighiero e Boetti's "Maps of the World." They shared an unshakeable belief in beauty, in overflow, in everythingness, the bursting, indelible beauty in a world where there is so much suffering and wounding and pain.

Eight

And so the story ends, or pauses, for as we know it is all one long story.

My sons and I have moved to New York City. Today we look out our window at the Hudson River and wait for another hurricane as the sky turns lavender and orange, Ficre colors. When the rain is most dramatic, we feel him close. The boys grow taller than everyone around them and become young men. Their grandfather turns eighty and with my mother they circle the wagons and leave their home of forty-two years in Washington, DC, where I grew up, and return to New York—their ancestral metropolis—to be extended family with us, as Ficre always wanted it.

New York is the place that called Ficre as well, a place with mythos, and a place where everyone belongs. Now I live in a neighborhood of stage doors and students walking down the street with huge instrument cases. The dancers pirouette on Lincoln Center Plaza and clatter down the street in high fabulosity. They are the children, making art. Ficre was one of the children, at the Art Students League, but he was never a child and always a child. That rare combination, true to his position on the zodiac. Ancient and brand-new, as anyone who knew him would say.

I am in New York City, where I was born, where I have spent decades trying to return. "Welcome home," I am told many times, even by people who do not know I was born in Harlem, USA, at 135 and Fifth, in the Riverton apartments, at Columbia Presbyterian Hospital, where my father was also born. Ficre and I never made it here together—that was planned for when the children graduated from high school.

Death sits in the comfortable chair in the corner of my new bedroom, smoking a cigarette. It is a he, sinuous and sleek, wearing a felt brimmed hat. He is there when I wake in the middle of the night, sitting quietly, his smoke a visible curl in the New York lights that come in between the venetian blind slats.

At first I am startled to see him. He sits so near, is so at home. But he doesn't move towards me, he simply co-habits. And so, eventually, I return to sleep. He isn't going anywhere, but he isn't going to take me, either. In the morning, the chair is empty.

Which is stronger, death sitting in the corner, or life in New York City? Death, or my teenage sons, sleeping profoundly in the next room, growing overnight? "I love plans!" my new friend Esther exults, and so do I, for nowadays I feel like plans are all that stands between me and the end of my life. I'm not going to die overnight because next Wednesday I am going with Esther to see an auction of nineteenth-century American documents at Swann Galleries. I'm not going to die tonight because I already took the chicken out of the freezer and Simon loves roast chicken and rice for dinner, and I promised him I would make it. I'm not going to die tonight because on Saturday Farah and I are bundling up and going for a walk against the blustery winds along the river, to continue the conversation we began almost thirty years ago when we were both in graduate school, before I even knew my beloved Ficre.

At the fish market, I see the very first sets of roe and flats of shad. Each year I make a ritual spring meal of shad and its roe, as my mother always did. I fry bacon crispy, pour out the grease but leave the pan slick, dredge the fragile, bloody roe in flour, salt, and pepper, and fry it in the bacon pan with onions while the shad broils. I serve it with buttered, parslied boiled new potatoes and steamed asparagus.

The first time I made this dish for Ficre he looked with suspicion at the roe. He knew it wasn't one of the bottom-feeding shellfish his religion forbade eating in his childhood, along with pork, but I'd gotten him over that and onto Team Bacon. His curiosity always won over habit, and he was fascinated by watching the glossy meat turn brown, and the feel of the egg sacs popping in his mouth. It reminded me of the liver I never liked before he made it for me during my fist pregnancy when I craved meat, blood and its necessary iron. He made it with garlic and berbere and olive oil, cooked it in strips that turned crisp, and tossed with lots of parsley.

"It's not easy to die, sweetie," Ficre used to say to me, when I'd have night terrors and wake in a panic. "I've seen people survive, and I know." I'd always had bad dreams and his words and presence were all that ever calmed me down, *It's not easy to die*; life force is actually mighty, and I have life force. It is not indelible, but it can behave like it is. We all die, but we don't die easily.

Though it seemed he slipped away, it could not have been easy. The heart inside of him beat all the beats it was allocated, but in his fifty years, the man lived. Not nearly enough, but not insufficiently. He found his life's work thrice: as an activist; as a chef; and as a painter. He understood himself as something larger than himself: His mighty, extended family of origin; his beloved native land and its people. He found love and became part of a new extended family, and a new people. He had children and made family, most important of all to him.

A statue of Frederick Douglass stands at the quiet Seventy-seventh Street entrance of the New York Historical Society, tall and mighty. He is someone who journeyed to freedom, I think, and I was married to someone who walked to freedom. The culmination of the freedom was love and family. That's all he did, that's what he did.

I hear my voice to my children, your father walked to freedom.

At my father's eightieth birthday I tell the room that when Ficre and I met, he told me he was not interested in anyone who did not love and honor her parents. He found too much of that in America.

In New York I feel joy overwhelming, and this same gratitude, for Ficre brought me here, I am sure of it, as sure as if he whispered in my ear, "Go, Lizzy. You are so much braver than you realize. Take the children and go."

What are the odds, we used to say, what are the odds, that we would end up in the same place and fall in love? Once upon a time, halfway around the world, two women were pregnant at the same time in very different places, and their children grew up and found each other. It happens every day.

Nine

The last music he listened to at home was Yusef Lateef's "The Plum Blossom." It filled our home beginning the Sunday morning after his birthday. Even after he died, there were birthday present ribbons left in the living room. The music was a gift from Marcus, and Ficre played it over and over that sweet Sunday. The sound was delicate and essential, a single pipe note, a blue note, something impending and then sudden, like spring rain. It took its time. And then in came the piano, ever so slightly percussive. The sounds layered and built into a quietly mighty sound. Lateef played varied instruments from different global music traditions, strands of a unified sound. You hear him actually breathe into the bamboo flute and hear his palm on the drum. The music repeated is the warm and human breath in our house that Sunday.

For many years Ficre tended a Natal plum bonsai. We bought it in a shop in Portsmouth, New Hampshire, on the way home from a happy trip to Maine. It was a South African variety, which amused us when we happened upon it in New Hampshire. Africa is everywhere, baby, he said, with a smile. It was spiky and flowerless. For two years Ficre nipped and shaped it, watered it, talked to it to coax it into health and bloom. He insisted it live on the kitchen table, in the center of our lives.

One morning we came downstairs and the whole first floor was suffused with a rare and lovely smell. The bonsai had burst its first small, waxy pink blossom. It scented our home and bloomed for several weeks. Orchids would die and I'd throw them away, but he'd set them in the basement to patiently wait for a blossom. "Africans are patient, Lizzy," he'd say, with a chuckle, but he meant it.

Ficre's books: Chinese philosophy, organic gardening, Roman antiquity, Paul Cézanne, Hadrian's Wall, African alphabets. When I was with him, I felt that there was suddenly enough time: to talk, to read, to think, to sleep, to make love, to drink coffee or tea, to practice yoga, to walk. I think that everyone felt that there was all the time in the world when they were with him.

We shared days I can only call divine. I don't want to fix that last Sunday as the most significant Sunday, though one cannot help but do so. I think of my friend Melvin Dixon—also gone too soon, from AIDS, at forty-two—and his poem "Fingering the Jagged Grains," a call and response that I took into my body. "What did I do?" I called to my village. The answer came, "*You lived, you lived*, and the jagged grains, so black and blue, opened like lips about to sing."

Ten

New York friends who loved Ficre come over to welcome us to our new home. We eat and laugh and drink and play music. Afterwards I am so tired that I sleep unguardedly.

Ficre comes to my dreams and has never been more vivid.

He is excited: he has just been named the chef in the historical division of a great art museum. He is to invent dishes, and to match pigments in paintings to their proper historical sources. He tells me the history of ocher: ferric oxide, an impure clay, makes the color, explains why it is red in Eritrea and yellow in southern France. The things he knew! How to make paper with suminagashi paper technique. Where there was a foundry in the Hudson Valley to do lost wax casting in bronze. How to butcher an entire lamb, and clean a fresh chicken. How to marbleize paper and make tiny notebooks with covers the pink, gray, and greens of some remembered quarry.

He loved that I was an American girl: tall, sturdy, sunny, good teeth, optimistic, full of songs from the Negro canon and the great American songbook. He loved my blues, which saw the world but never laid me low. He knew more than I did that we were not meant to survive if not to profit for others, and that I came from survivors.

Later that morning, I ask my sons: how can we be so happy, when we have been through so much? The forest is not denuded. The trees are standing tall.

In the dream, he picks up my coffee cup and examines it; I have purchased it since he died; he finds the curve of the handle and pale pink, crackled glaze to be beautiful. *Sit with me, darling*, he says, *and have a cup of coffee.*

Eleven

I dream we are moving, my family of four: Lizzy, Ficre, Solomon, and Simon.

It is light and easy. We laugh with the boys as we sort through and throw things away. Ficre carries and moves large bags and objects, the African ox, sturdy and purposeful. The boys move as oxen as well. We are glad to be going wherever we are going.

Then the children evaporate from the dreamscape and it is just the two of us walking a long, gently curved road, holding hands. At a fork in the road, Ficre lets my hand go and waves me on. You have to keep walking, Lizzy, he says. I know it is the only truth, so I walk.

I look back. I look back. I can still see him, smiling and waving me on.

It was the two of us walking the road and now he has let my hand go.

I walk. I can always see him. His size does not change as I move forward: he is five foot nine and a half, exactly right. I can still feel the feel of my hand in his hand as I walk.

I wake and the room is flooded with pale yellow light.

Notes from the Road:
An Afterward Moving Forward

I never imagined that when I wrote first one word and then another in the wake of the sudden loss of my husband that I was beginning the process of writing a memoir, let alone a memoir that would make its way into the world and connect me to so many people and stories. Braced by my writing hand on the dining room table, I felt I was literally making sounds, not even words, one by one, until they became fragments, then sentences, and then something whole that told me not what I was feeling but rather what was happening, at the most basic level. "The earth will hold me," I would remind myself as I wrote between sentences I was alive and I was a mother, and I could think and breathe and write, even as I felt the earth had been swept out from beneath me. Such was the state in which I began *The Light of the World*. When I finished it— after sharing it with my sons, for I would not have put it forth in the world without their assent—I did not feel it had been cathartic, as many quite reasonably asked me. But I knew I had written my way through a stretch in the road of my life, and that each word was a necessary step forward to the next station, the next stage, brief poet's chapter by brief chapter.

When the book was first excerpted in *The New Yorker* a deluge of email began to come to me which continued a few months later when the book was published and then again as I set out on the road. The book seemed to ask for a tour that was a little bit different from the usual. As much as *The Light of the World* is a love story that begins with two people and tells a particular story about a particular man, and family, I wanted those particulars to radiate outward and be meaningful in ever-widening circles. For loss is our common denominator. None of us will escape it. None of us will outrun death. What do we do in the space between that is our lives? What is the quality and richness of our lives? How do we move through struggle and let community hold us when we have been laid low? This book had to live someplace outside of the sound of my own voice, to paraphrase the poet Sekou Sundiata, another dear one gone too soon. It had to be larger than me and my individual love.

Many things happened on the road that were profound. I might have expected to connect with other widows who read the book and connected because of demographic commonalities. But I found the human connections far exceeded that boundary. In Los Angeles, I did a reading with a group called "Inside/Out Writing" that creates writing workshops for incarcerated young people and then continues that writing practice when they are released, both as an anti-recidivism method and also to continue to build community. I read with some of those young people who shared stories that they wrote through. Two of them interviewed me with tremendous care and closed the interview by thanking me in their languages—Tagalog and Korean—recasting Ficre's polyglot mantra that I described in the book: What could be more important than saying thank you in someone's original language? A young man who joined the program while a teenager in prison gave me a bag filled with glitter in which was a tiny glass bottle with a cork plug. The plug was a computer drive, and his own poems jumped up on my screen when I plugged it in, a life in verse, someone else who was moving forward with writing.

And some connections took me beyond Ficre and were merely moving, or uncanny. Among the moving: the man who came up to me and told me he was so happy to have found me because it connected him to my father, who was a childhood playmate of his. Their parents had been united in the wish for justice and connection between blacks and Jews, and he inherited my father's childhood wooden boat, a picture of which he brought me; his own grandchildren now play with it. Ficre would have loved that, and so I showed my father a picture of a beloved childhood toy he had not laid eyes on in 70 years. Stories carry memory, and connect.

Or the Haitian poet who spoke to me of the many commonalities and of the figure of the horseman that Ficre was painting at the time of his passing being a harbinger of death. I will never know if Ficre had foreknowledge of his passing—nor would I wonder, nor would it matter, given the intractable fact of his death—but I am stirred by the idea that from another culture, someone saw symbol and ritual and meaning and was moved by it.

A colleague, a classicist, after hearing me read in New Haven wrote to me:

When I read your achingly lyrical account of Ficre's last days and the hawk, taken as an omen, that prompted the acrostic and lottery tickets, it made me imagine that, somehow, feelingly, at a subconscious level your husband had an intuition of disquiet and danger ahead. And I find it very moving that he responded by trying to turn the apparition into a propitious omen for his family (the urge to win the lottery for you on page 24). Now whenever I read passages where Homeric warriors prophesy on the cusp of death I will think of your book and of its hero, Ficre.

I received this interpretation of the Jewish Kabbalah poems I heard of hearing in the minutes before Ficre died:

I believe that what we are uniquely given, as humans, windows into the infinity of God. We are also given the remarkable ability to open our windows wider, to stretch our view into the infinite—worship, beckoning, weeping, joy, bearing, birth, banjo, love, poetry, astrophysics, term papers, painting, a hawk devouring a squirrel. To me, this is what you describe in your story, the stretching of your world, the ability to see and experience and love more deeply as you built a life together with Ficre and your sons, to join your windows from such different worlds together so you could all peer more deeply into the infinite.

But you are never going to get all the way there—because that is the nature of infinity. You were never going to have your husband and lover forever, no one can. What you were and are able to do, and what you express so beautifully, is to deeply appreciate the additional depths and dimensions you were able to reach because of the time you had with him, and the sons you had together, and the new windows into the infinite that opened for you.

and he saw—
windows without number and end.

As a writer, it is so very rare to have someone tell you what they see in your work and expand it into a different world. Sometimes—oftentimes—our writing has meaning in it that we didn't even put there. "The poem is smarter than the poet," we poets often say, which is to note: we dredge so much from the subconscious for our work that we cannot even be aware or sure of all we put in it. So the gift, rarely glimpsed, is what others see there, and thus what was and is within us.

On the book tour and in the letters I have had the privilege of receiving, people/readers have shared with me very, very intimate stories, each of which I have held like treasures, of loss, and family, and its simultaneous strength and vulnerability. The strength of human connection gets us through this life, but we are also, in moments of profound loss, reminded of how fragile this life is. How do you start again and carry the past within you? Why is it important to carry that with us? What remains when the body is no longer here? I have been privileged on this journey to be able to contemplate and respond those questions. My readers and audiences have helped me.

Writer after writer has talked about how we are connected by stories, that what makes us human or where we measure our humanness is in a long chain of stories. Word to word, word as piece of soul, soul to soul. I believe that now as never before.

I found that first-generation Americans connected with the story of what I had not previously thought of as a mixed marriage, American and immigrant. And that they saw in Ficre's life story not the tragedy of his passing, but a wonderful way to make a new life in America, to work hard and aspire to be not just a doctor or an engineer as so many hard-working parents would wish for their children but rather, an artist, someone uniquely positioned to tell the tale and exemplify their life of cross-culture. To tell the tale of what happens when you come from one place and make something new in glorious combination in America.

At every reading, someone of course would ask, how are the boys? Solo and Simon were twelve and thirteen when they lost their father; when this paperback comes out, four years after Ficre's passing, they will be almost seventeen and eighteen. Solo will have just graduated high school and Simon will be commencing his senior year. I am truly in awe of their courage, and every day is graced by their even-headedness, sense of purpose, and hilarity. They are joyful young people. Their father is with them and with us but I think that having survived tragedy, they have realized that they and we are strong enough to weather it, and that the world is lit by a million exciting things every day. I see their father in them physically, and also my father and their uncles on both sides. Mostly, they are themselves.

It is not easy to go back to the site of a book like this and write about it. Writing in the very wake of my husband's sudden passing was writing in a zone. The language there was raw and true and lit; there was urgency. I knew as I wrote that I would not be the same person on the other side. The Rilke I quoted in the book continues to resonate for me: "No feeling is final." Never have I so clearly understood life and the road to be walked. And while I write in the book of hearing "Mahalia Jackson as though for the first time," I also hear anew "Will the Circle be Unbroken," for so many circles have been drawn in the life of this book, a life that is certainly bigger than mine or even that of the mighty, beautiful, soulful Ficre, the most beautiful person anyone ever knew. This book was not a conjurer's wand to bring him back to life. But he lives in its pages, and like other heroes of literature, he teaches us something about how to live our days in detail. Every day can have beauty and tenderness, at the simplest level of the meal and a flower in a garden. Every day can contain some small pleasure. Every act can have integrity, be courageous, and be guided by kindness. Over and over again as I met people who themselves had been refugees or suffered political consequences in different countries, I think of the courage to start anew, and the miracle of positivity and light.

In simplicity is such guiding truth. I turn again to the spirituals. "This little light of mine, I'm gonna let it shine" could also be an epigraph to this book, if it were not understood as being simply a merry exhortation. It was, after all, best known as an anthem during the mighty struggles of the civil rights movement. That beautifully repeated let it shine, let it shine, let it shine performs the will to live in the context of mighty, life-and-death struggle. The word "shine" is bright radiance itself.

This book existed in my own body and now it connects and continues to connect with others, making an ever-widening human circle. Our individual lights are small compared to all the light in the world. More light. More light.

Acknowledgments

Before this book could be written or even imagined, my sons and I had to be put back together again in the wake of Ficre's loss. My parents, Clifford and Adele Alexander, took care of us in every way, putting our needs above and before their own and standing tall and steady by our sides. They teach me how to be mighty every day. My brother, Mark Alexander, and his family gave unwavering loving support. Ficre's amazing extended family all over the world showed their love and regard for him in many ways. Father Peter Orfanakos of St. Barbara Greek Orthodox Church kindly and patiently taught me many things I never knew I'd need to know, as did Mr. William Cameron at the Grove Street Cemetery. Monica Negrón, Lisa Gaither, Jomaire Crawford, Lisa Marcus, Ken Marcus, Lin Song, and Tyler McCauley helped me stay whole, each in their own way.

My colleagues at Yale University were compassionate and kind beyond measure. Rick and Jane Levin, Regina Starolis, Jonathan Holloway, Emilie Townes, Peter Salovey, and

Marta Moret extended special courtesies from the university community. Glenda Gilmore immediately took over my chairship of the African American Studies Department in the first weeks when I could not work; Lisa Monroe, Janet Giarratano, and Jodie Stewart-Moore held down the departmental fort. Each of my faculty colleagues in my beloved community of the African American Studies Department showed me how fortunate it is to work with people you also love. Our dear graduate students in African American studies brought home-made food to our home every night at five thirty for weeks: Thank you, my dears. Other special friends outside of the department who were especially helpful in their steady kindness include Steve Pitti and Alicia Schmidt Camacho, Inderpal Grewel, Joseph Gordon, Chip Long, Jon Butler, Jock Reynolds, George Chauncey, and Ron Gregg.

Helen Kauder, Key Jo Lee, Kathryn Kaelin, Kristin Graves, Lily Sawyer-Kaplan, Lulu Chua-Rubenfeld, Heather Vermuelen, Kenny Rivera, and Ronny Quevedo helped me immeasurably with bringing Ficre's artwork into the world and keeping it protected. Key Jo Lee, especially, entered the world of what Ficre saw head-first and lovingly catalogued and cared for the work. Her contribution was epic, as well as exquisitely professional.

My neighbors were true, especially Mike and Stephanie O'Malley, Martha Venter, Inderpal Grewel and Alfred Jessell, Heather Gerken and David Simon, Owen and Irene Fiss, Karin Render, and Thach Pham. The entire community at St. Thomas's Day School under the leadership of Fred Acquavita rallied around us, even though my sons had graduated from the school. At Hopkins School I would like to especially thank Errol Saunders for his ongoing kindness and understanding, as well as Michael Van Leesten and Lisa McGrath, and JoAnn Wich, who taught my sons to open their mouths and make a joyful noise.

For my family of friends who have loved and cared for us in a million ways: Alondra Nelson, Farah Griffin and Obery Hendricks, Miriam Gohara and Marcus McFerren, Tracey Meares, Jason Moran and Alicia Hall-Moran, Kellie Jones, Guthrie Ramsey, and Hettie Jones, James Forman and Ify Nwokoye, Kica Matos and Henry Fernandez, Amy Chua and Jed Rubenfeld, Anne Higonnet and John Geanakoplos, Michael Kaplan and Susan Sawyer, Geraldine and Suzanne Artis, Amy Cappellazzo and Joanne Rosen, Mona and Rashid Khalidi, Ann Marie and David Wilkins, John Gennari and Emily Bernard, Cindy Carter Cole, Kate and Gerald Chertavian, Jennifer DeVere Brody, Anna Deavere Smith, Darryk Floyd, Robin Coste Lewis, Esther Fein, Hilton Als. I could not begin to list all you have done for us. I cherish you as family.

A few friends in my community of writers have been particularly constructive and encouraging. Thank you to Nicky Dawidoff, Hilton Als, Kevin Young, Terrance Hayes, and Caryl Phillips. As they say, all faults contained here are my own.

Thanks to the Provost's office at Yale University for the sabbatical year in which this book was written, to Louise Mirrer at the New York Historical Society for providing me a workspace, and to Valerie Paley there for welcoming me. Thanks also to my colleague David Blight who insisted I have, and helped me find, this "room of one's own."

Faith Childs has been my agent since my first book of poems was published in 1990. She has been a steadfast champion of my work through thick and thin and has guided and supported my career for now three decades with brilliant professionalism. For this book, she was more intimately involved than ever before; I needed her there at every step and borrowed her stability and calm when the writing—and the journey to get to it—was especially difficult and dark. Thank you, Faith.

Gretchen Young, Jamie Raab, and Deb Futter at Grand Central envisioned this book before I did, dared to ask for it, and have fully supported and encouraged it all the way. This book truly would not have existed without Grand Central, and I am proud and grateful to be published here.

More gratitude for Gretchen Young, an editor of my dreams, wise and patient, laser-clear, whose steadfast support and uncanny understanding of this book brought me all the way to the finish line.

If I have neglected to mention anyone, please forgive my lapse. The bounty of help I accepted over this period is without measure, and sometimes help made its way through a thick fog. There is so much love and generosity in the world.

Finally, to Solomon Kebede Ghebreyesus and Simon Alexander Ghebreyesus, whose character, heart, resilience, courage, and humor leave me awe-struck. Their love makes me whole. Their constant encouragement enabled me to write and finish this book, and I thank them for allowing me to write about them, and about our precious, private family life. They carry the exquisite best of their father. For you, Solo and Simon, I reserve my most profound and undying gratitude. Of course, my darlings, this book is for you.

Questions for Elizabeth Alexander

1. As a poet, your lyricism seems to carry over to your prose writing. Do you have a different approach to writing prose from your poetry? Why did you choose the medium of a memoir in this case? Have you also been writing poems about Ficre, about your loss?

I believe that poets always write "as poets," with utmost attention to each word, the rhythms of the writing, and its musicality. For this book in particular, I was keenly aware that the writing came from the same "place" within me where poetry resides, somewhere lyrical and partially unknown such that the process of writing is a process of revelation. I didn't choose this form, it chose me—for exploring this zone of intense love and grieving, as well as for the indelible force of life and its power and beauty, gave me something new on the hopefully long journey of my artistic development.

2. What guided the structure of this memoir? Can you speak to the memoir's sense of time?

I wrote one small section at a time, as I would write poems, and then when enough of them had accrued, I began working with the small pieces to find the shape for the larger whole. As a poet and as a writer of critical essays I am not wired to "write long," but bit by bit, the pieces made a whole. The space between the chapters functions as a pause, like the white space after stanzas or between poems in a collection. I didn't want to "bury the lead," so I thought it important to tell, up front, the story of my husband's sudden passing, in real time. But then it seemed inevitable that in order for the reader to continue to care about the characters and stay engaged with us that I needed to talk about love, and falling in love, and the rich years that Ficre and I spent creating a family around shared political, artistic, and domestic values, augmented by devotion to home and family, blood and chosen.

3. Can you tell us a little about your life since you completed the memoir? How did you guide your loved ones through such a difficult transition? How has your role as a mother changed since then?

Two and a half years after losing our beloved Ficre, I find it amazing that my sons and I have moved our lives to New York (though I continue to teach at Yale), that they are thriving in school, family, city life, that I have finished a memoir I am proud of, and that we are standing tall. I don't actually know how I did it except to say that I have always been taught to be strong and ready, and to call upon "the village," however far-flung. I have drawn even closer to my sons and spend as much time as possible with them, listening to them and continuing our family life, keeping the memory of their father alive while also stepping into the light of the future. A few months after Ficre died I said to myself, with surprise, "You are a single mother!" I have always had great respect for women who do the tough, full-time job of child-rearing alone, and when you are used to doing it with a highly engaged partner, as Ficre was, it's a real adjustment. There's just more to attend to and more responsibility, and I deeply miss the intimate shared processing of my children's lives. So life needs to be quite organized. I have a lot of support. And it is a daily privilege and joy to mother my two extraordinary sons.

4. Were there books or works of art that you turned to in the process of writing this memoir?

For a long time I didn't read anything, couldn't read. I felt I had no room to take in anything that would make my brain and emotions work harder. Reading would have made me feel more than I could bear, it seemed. That changed with Tony Judt's *The Memory Chalet*, wherein he chronicles the vivid dream and memory life that persists even as he is essentially immobilized by Lou Gehrig's Disease (A.L.S.). I then tried to stay away from books that were explicitly memoirs of loss, because I didn't want to unconsciously borrow anything. But Edwidge Danticat's memoir *Brother, I'm Dying* stayed important to me, about filial love and loss in a family dealing with the vagaries of the immigration system. I also spent a lot of time with the poetry of Lucille Clifton and Rainier Maria Rilke, poetry that was emotionally knowing, clear and true, and attendant to the mysteries of life at the same time. I found—and still find—I craved music of all kinds, as often as possible. I want to be flooded with music because it makes me feel alive, beyond words.

5. What would you tell someone in their twenties who wants to be in a relationship?

I would tell them that you really never know when love is around the corner, so be alert to what life offers you. I would tell them to find love by being their best selves, enriching themselves, exploring the activities and ideas they love. I would tell them that once you are in a relationship love is a garden that needs tending, corny but true. And I would tell them that if you love and then lose a person—as we all do in some way or another—you do not lose the love you were given and participated in. It is indelible.

About the Author

ELIZABETH ALEXANDER composed and recited "Praise Song for the Day" for President Barack Obama's 2009 inauguration. She is the author of six books of poetry—including *American Sublime*, a finalist for the Pulitzer Prize—and is the first winner of the Jackson Prize for Poetry and a National Endowment for the Arts and Guggenheim fellow. She is the Wun Tsun Tam Mellon Professor in the Humanities at Columbia University and serves as a Chancellor of the Academy of American Poets. For more information, visit ElizabethAlexander.net.